The Changing Landscape of Labor

AMERICAN WORKERS AND WORKPLACES

Photographs by Michael Jacobson-Hardy

Essays by John T. Cumbler and Robert E. Weir

Foreword by Bruce Laurie

UNIVERSITY OF MASSACHUSETTS PRESS   *Amherst*

This book was published in conjunction with the exhibition *The Changing Landscape of Labor: American Workers and Workplaces* at the University of Massachusetts at Amherst, University Gallery, Fine Arts Center, 1996.

All rights reserved
LC 95–17443
ISBN 0–87023–983–X
Designed by Mary Mendell
Set in ITC Berkeley Oldstyle
Printed and bound in Singapore
Library of Congress Cataloging-in-Publication Data
Jacobson-Hardy, Michael, 1951–
    The changing landscape of labor: American workers and workplaces
  / photographs by Michael Jacobson-Hardy; essays by John T. Cumbler
  and Robert E. Weir; foreword by Bruce Laurie.
      p.   cm.
    Includes bibliographical references.
    ISBN 0–87023–983–X
    1. Labor—New England—History—20th century—Pictorial works.
  2. Manual work—New England—History—20th century—Pictorial works.
  3. Working class—New England—History—20th century—Pictorial
  works. 4. Factories—New England—History—20th century—Pictorial
  works. 5. Documentary photography—History.   I. Cumbler, John T.
  II. Weir, Robert E., 1952– .   III. Title.
  HD8083.A11J33   1995
  331.2'0974—dc20   95–17443
                                                                                            CIP

British Library Cataloguing in Publication data are available.

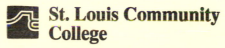

THE CHANGING LANDSCAPE OF LABOR

Contents

Acknowledgments

In 1989, I began photographing and interviewing blue collar workers in many New England industries. I believe that their voices must be heard and that their ideas are important to any discussion about the restructuring of industry and society so that work is both valued and paid for, and that those who make the things which we count on are valued and respected for their contributions. I am indebted to the many workers who took time to participate in this project. In addition, I would like to thank Bruce Laurie, John Cumbler, and Robert Weir for their essays. I would like to especially thank Bruce Wilcox and Clark Dougan at the University of Massachusetts Press for their continued support over the two years it took to complete this book. I am grateful to the museum directors with whom I have had the good fortune to work, including Betsy Siersma at the University Gallery at the University of Massachusetts, Hollister Sturgess at the Springfield Museum of Fine Arts, and Wendy Watson at the Mount Holyoke College Art Museum. Thanks to Patricia Greenfield and the staff of the University of Massachusetts Labor Relations and Research Center and Stuart Kaufman at the George Meany Memorial Archives. The Lowell Central Labor Council, the Pioneer Valley Central Labor Council, UAW Local 2322, the Massachusetts AFL-CIO and the National AFL-CIO made generous contributions. I want to thank the staff at the Lowell National Historical Park and the Massachusetts Heritage State Parks for displaying the exhibition in its early stages. Thanks to the Massachusetts Foundation for the Humanities for their initial project support plus the Holyoke Arts Council, a local agency, the Massachusetts Cultural Council, a state agency, and the National Endowment for the Arts, and the

Eastman Kodak Professional Photography Division plus the Agfa Photo Division. This project was made possible with additional funds from Berkshire Electric Cable Company, Sunoco Products Company, Parsons Paper Company, University Products, Inc., T. Mark Futter, and Gladys and Paul Jacobson. Thanks to my wife, Ruth, for her ongoing support and belief in my work.

Michael Jacobson-Hardy

viii   *Acknowledgments*

Foreword

BRUCE LAURIE

This splendid book rewards its reader twice over, with the thoughtful essays of historians John Cumbler and Robert Weir and with the remarkable photographs of Michael Jacobson-Hardy. This is no place to anticipate the discussions of Cumbler and Weir. It is enough to say that each supplies context to help us understand both the development of social documentary photography and the pattern of industrial change in New England, birthplace of the industrial revolution in the early nineteenth century and of the recent "high-tech revolution." It is appropriate, however, to comment on Jacobson-Hardy's arresting images.

It can no longer be said, as the early photographer and social reformer Jacob Riis did just about a century ago, that one-half of the nation does not know how the other half lives. Thanks to proliferation of news sources in different media, along with our mix of morbid fascination with and fear of the homeless, most of us have a rough sense of what life is like for the swelling throng of castoffs in our urban centers. And thanks to our ongoing curiosity about the "rich and famous," we no longer puzzle over the doings of the wealthy. For all the criticism aimed at modern journalism, it has at least given us a clearer image of the well-to-do and the poor. The glaring omission is the manual worker, the men and women who make the things that help make modern life what it is. We all know what they produce and why a growing roster of American goods stands in danger of being overwhelmed by foreign imports. Every American instantly recognizes the latest name-brand sneaker, audio system, or automobile. Very few, however, have ever seen an image of such products in the making.

The opaque quality of the factory hand is not new. It traces to the origins of the industrialization in the opening decade of the nineteenth century. Between then and the l890s, and increasingly after the Civil War, publishers sometimes commissioned artists to illustrate books and articles on the industrial scene with sketches of workers, machines, or factories. The invention of the daguerreotype in the late 1830s opened new and exciting possibilities in graphic artistry. Early photographers quickly perfected the genre of the "occupational daguerreotype," which typically captured a tradesman bearing the dress and tools of his craft. These, of course, were highly stylized portraits composed in studios, not shots of workers on the job. Such candid work awaited the photographic breakthroughs of the Civil War, which gave us pictures of miners and railroad workers on the job in the West, as well as the more familiar battlefront fare. Yet for all the artistic innovation in this period of war and accelerated industrialism it was the rare photographer who ventured into the sooty factories and grim garrets of the city. Not until Jacob Riis and then Lewis Hine turned their lens on the "other half," Robert Weir reminds us, did we finally get to see the ordinary people of urban America at work and play. Why this is so isn't entirely clear. Perhaps turn-of-the-century Americans let their Victorian abomination of manual work get the best of them. Possibly they considered the working class a social threat, and the factory too private a place for meddlesome photographers. Maybe they simply weren't interested. No matter. With this extraordinary volume Jacobson-Hardy, like Riis and Hine before him, helps rescue the industrial worker from the dark. He illuminates a corner of experience we would rather not see or have done our best to ignore, all the more so now that the typical industrial worker is likely to bear the stigma of poverty, gender, or race, or all three. In that respect Jacobson-Hardy's photos speak for themselves, and they speak eloquently indeed.

Social documentarians like Jacobson-Hardy have historically been spearheads for change, genteel reformers in stiff collars whose galvanic images proved invaluable props for consumer advocates, environmentalists, and labor activists. Whether his work will have the impact of a Riis or Hine, of course, remains to be seen. Prospects do not seem promising today. The labor movement is a diminished force adrift in hostile seas. Employers and politicians resist reform in full view of an indifferent public. Labor's traditional allies in the liberal center, moreover, have deserted, and its comrades on the left are in disarray. One could have made similar observations, however, on the eve of the Progressive Era and the New Deal, the two great outbursts of reform in the twentieth century that improved conditions for working people on and off the job. Such moments should warn against using the past or the present to predict the future. History simply tells us what was, not what will be.

We can be more confident that in the immediate future at least Jacobson-Hardy's workers are likely to confront the same uncertainty and economic insecurity that they have known for the last two decades. As John Cumbler astutely observes, some of these are older workers using dated equipment in seedy mills and shops with a bleak future or no future at all. The rest are younger operatives, often women, who work in settings that are recognizably modern but not necessarily of a piece with the pervasive image of the computerized factory. The last photos in this volume imply that for all the talk of the obsolescence of manual work in the new "knowledge-based economy," even the most computer-age factories continue to be labor-intensive workplaces dependent on human intervention.

Whether labor intensive or not, industrial work in the United States falls into a troubling pattern. Growing numbers of jobs pay subsistence wages and carry few if any benefits, either because they are part-time or because employers cannot or will not offer pensions, medical coverage, and other social provisions. This mocks the adage so popular with the post-World War II generation that a job is the best social program. The irony is that poor wages and slim benefit packages have become compelling arguments not for the elimination of social programs, but for the expansion of existing policies and the development of new ones, including some form of national health insurance.

This new industrial system also suggests that we have inadvertently slipped into a sort of social experiment that will test whether general prosperity is possible without a strong manufacturing base, and an industrial work force schooled in the ways of the shop and paid enough income to support a decent standard of living. It should come as no surprise that the "experts" are of mixed minds. Some welcome low-wage production as a blessing that enhances American competitiveness in international markets; others condemn it as morally indefensible and economically dangerous. That this debate is not merely academic should be clear to any reader of this book.

As for the workers themselves, Jacobson-Hardy catches them at their most vulnerable. The older machine operators among them are not simply a class in decline, but a class threatened with extinction—possibly the last Americans to make tangible things in any quantity. They represent an older America whose boast was a skilled and resourceful industrial working class that enjoyed the highest standard of living in the world. We find them here rich in dignity and in manual skills that are foolishly squandered with each plant closing.

From Bolts of Cotton to Hamburgers:
The Deindustrialization of New England

JOHN T. CUMBLER

On July 24, 1882, Theodore Lyman, a wealthy Boston philanthropist and investor, made a speech in Dedham in favor of his candidacy for Congress as an independent Mugwump reformer. When someone in the audience asked about his support of the tariff, Lyman reminded his listeners of the importance of manufacturing to the state whose soil was notoriously rocky and infertile. "As long as Massachusetts was overlaid by 10 feet of gravel, she would have to manufacture or starve."[1] Although manufacturing did produce "manufacturing towns with their humming machinery, their prosaic faces, their long hard streets, ugly buildings, and sickly smells," which were "deadening to the soul," without it the state could not "be a great and intellectual" region.[2] It would have "no mills and no dams, nothing but a few grist-mills here and there and houses whose occupants raised such crops as they could from the scanty soil." The state would be "poor" and "stupid also."[3]

Theodore Lyman grew up in the era of great industrial expansion for Massachusetts and benefited disproportionately from it. His father, an early mayor of Boston, and his grandfather before that, made a fortune in overseas trade, then in the 1820s shifted their investments to the Boston Associates' textile mills. Lyman, born in 1833 when the textile centers of northern New England fueled the state's initial burst of industrial growth, had seen Massachusetts' industrial economy diversify and his personal wealth grow. "I am not an old man, and yet when I think of the state of our manufacturing in my boyhood and when I look at

From Bolts of Cotton to Hamburgers

John T. Cumbler

them today, I can hardly believe my eyes such is the enormous growth in variety, in technical skill, and in inventive power."[4]

Indeed by the time Lyman ran for Congress in 1882, the state's textile mills employed 58,365 persons in cotton and 26,000 in woolens and worsteds.[5] The early success of textiles encouraged the construction of dams and mills wherever New England rivers plummeted far enough to generate the water power for the machines that provided cheap durable fabric to clothe the farmers of the West as they broke the prairie sod, the factory worker in Pittsburgh and Chicago who produced the plows for those farmers, and the slaves (and later the freedmen) who produced the cotton for the hungry mills. But despite the great appetite of the domestic market for cotton cloth, New England mills and textile machines outpaced even that demand. By the 1850s the Holyoke dam opened up a new era of industrialization in western Massachusetts. This huge dam ran a fifth of a mile, although it was so large that it collapsed shortly after opening and had to be rebuilt. The new structure, and the accompanying canal system, was originally intended for textile mills. The tidy profits gained from Lowell had already encouraged the construction of mills in Manchester, New Hampshire and later Lawrence, Massachusetts, as well as textile manufacturing in southeastern Massachusetts. The productive capacity of these mills had by midcentury far outstripped the market's ability to absorb the cloth. By the time Holyoke was developed as a factory town, on the model of Lowell, the textile industry had slacked off. The original development company went bankrupt but the natural resource and built structures remained. Soon other companies moved in to produce not only cottons and woolens but also paper and spool thread. By the 1880s, more than one-quarter of the state's 8,000 paper workers were in Holyoke.[6]

While mill agents and workers struggled over wages for weaving and spinning, cordwainers and merchant capitalists were transforming the process of shoe production along the East coast. As early as the 1830s, shoe bosses were breaking up the small shops where artisans and journeymen had worked. Cut leather was increasingly put out into the smaller shops of the town and the countryside to be worked for piece rate. By the time Lyman graduated from Harvard in 1855, shoe companies were hiring women to work on stitching machines in new factories behind the main streets of the eastern towns. If during his run for Congress he had visited a shoe factory, Lyman would have seen parts of shoes produced on a variety of machines, which in turn were produced in machine shops throughout the region. By the 1880s, 63,403 people were at work making shoes to shod farmers, factory workers, housewives, and seamstresses. Although shoes, textiles, and paper epitomized industrial New England, the region also boasted a significant iron and steel industry with 29,500 workers, mostly centered in Worcester. There were 5,176 rubber workers in towns like Holyoke; another 16,000 people worked in machine shops, transforming material into capital goods.[7] To a wealthy man such as Theodore Lyman, who lived on a comfortable suburban farm in Chestnut Hill, the "manufacturing towns [of Massachusetts] with their humming machinery, their prosaic faces, their long hard streets, ugly buildings, and sickly smells," were "deadening to the soul." But to their manual workers, they were home and places of work.[8] These industrial workers were often at odds with their employers over wages, but they also took pride in their labor, or in what Lyman saw as "the technical skill and . . . inventive power." Both the conflict and the pride gave impetus to trade unions, strikes, and petitions for shorter hours.[9]

The workers who found employment in "the ugly buildings" came from a variety of backgrounds. In Lyman's youth, the textile hands were largely women who for the most part came from New England's countryside.[10] Civil War casualties and westward and urban migration of young males further distorted the ratio of women to men in rural New England. Options were limited for single women in this setting. From stern and harsh work on farms, more and more women moved to the even more disciplined and taxing work of the mills. But there they found new female companionship and better wages than they could have made doing housework on the farms. New England females also found their way into the shoe shops of eastern Massachusetts as binders and later as machine stitchers, making a world that gave dignity to their labor.[11] In those shoe shops and mills, the women of New England shared work rooms with male factory workers and fellow rural New Englanders in flight from the decline of commercial and subsistence agriculture.[12]

By 1882, when Theodore Lyman went about eastern Massachusetts in his campaign for Congress, the complexion of the New England labor force had changed. The native population had aged and its families had shrunk.[13] Fewer and fewer rural New England women entered the mills and shops. Those who took their place were also men and women escaping declining commercial and subsistence agriculture, but by the 1880s these men and women were more likely to come from Quebec or Ireland. The proportion of the region's foreign-born population was close to 25 percent, one of the highest percentages in the country.[14] On their journey to Massachusetts they may have stopped first in the mill towns of Lancashire, or along the docks of Liverpool or London, or at the mills of Montreal. Whatever their route, they brought with them laboring customs and cultural traditions both similar and different from the workers they replaced at the looms or at the spinning, carding, stitching, and bleaching machines.[15] Their English was thick with Irish or French accents, their religion was Catholic, and they encountered hostility on shop floors and in communities. But the xenophobia of Yankee workers and employers did not stem the growing stream of immigrants in search of work. By the 1880s no other region in the country invested as much money per capita in manufacturing or had more industrial jobs. Although the work was hard, the hours long, and the pay low, there were jobs for the taking, which had not been true in Ireland or Quebec. The newcomers found hostility, but they also found solidarity.

By the time Theodore Lyman's family attended his funeral in 1897, many of the male Irish and French Canadian workers whom he had looked on with misgiving had moved into the skilled positions as loom fixers, mule spinners, lasters, and skilled machine tenders of the fourdrinier paper machines; the women had become proficient at weaving or machine stitching.[16] By the turn of the century, there were different, newer accents heard above the din of machinery in the mills and shops that continued to create the wealth of New England.

Emigrants from Portugal, Italy, Poland, Greece, Russia, and the Middle East competed for work in aging factory buildings. Like its factories, New England's native-born work force was also aging, but its ranks were being replenished by new emigrants from abroad.[17]

In the early years of the twentieth century, New England workers still wove most of the nation's cloth, stitched and lasted most of its shoes, and pressed most of its paper. With each passing year, however, Boston's shoppers were confronted with more cloth woven elsewhere, shoes finished in other states, and paper in boxes shipped from outside the Commonwealth. The owners of the mills of Lowell, Chicopee, Lawrence, and Fall River, whose homes looked out over the leafy avenues of Chestnut Hill, Newton, and Fall River were building new factories in North Carolina, Georgia, and Alabama. The machines in these new factories were still built in Massachusetts and financed by Yankee capital. The skilled mechanics who came down from New England to set up this equipment were working in the South with new rural mill folk.

Growing competition from new factories in the South and West, and even in rural New England, pressured workers in Massachusetts to increase their productivity and accept low wages, but competition did not reduce industrial employment in the Commonwealth. Through the early years of the twentieth century, New England manufacturing towns continued to absorb European immigrants. The skill of the New England workers, particularly the machine builders and tenders, encouraged manufacturers to invest in a variety of new manufacturing enterprises, which turned out weight scales, hardware, furnaces, stoves, toys, and sporting equipment for the growing American middle class.

The Great War brought this heady industrial production to a climax. Manufacturers ran at full production and paid high wages to meet wartime needs. But when the war ended, so did the first great industrial era of New England. Owners reinvested less and less capital in New England factories: machines grew older, and underutilized buildings grew shabby. By the mid-1920s shoes and textiles were in decline, and the manufacturers employed fewer workers and bought fewer machines. In 1926 North Carolina surpassed Massachusetts in production of cotton goods, and in 1929 South Carolina pushed Massachusetts into third place. New and more efficient electrified factories, many of them outside New England, used the latest machinery to produce more with a significantly smaller labor force. Nationwide employment shrunk in these industries, but New England was particularly hard hit. Employment in boot and shoes peaked in 1919 at more than 80,000 workers.[18] Between 1919 and 1929, Massachusetts' share of national shoe production dipped from 40 to 25 percent. By the end of the decade shoe production in the state had fallen 50 percent.[19] In 1919 Massachusetts produced 28 percent of the nation's cotton textiles, while fifteen years later it produced only 10.7 percent. Even with papermaking, which grew during the 1920s because of the dramatic growth in the paper-consuming service sector and financial activity, Massachusetts did not get its share of the growth.[20] Paper producers in Wisconsin and Maine, utilizing newer, more efficient equipment and plants, captured a larger share of this growth than did the older plants in the Connecticut River Valley.

In the key industries of the region, wages peeked in 1920 and declined for the rest of the decade. The wage differential between Massachusetts and the South declined in some job categories as the Bay State closed mills and the remaining workers faced wage cuts.[21] There was not much roaring in Massachusetts during the roaring twenties; mostly there was growing silence.[22] Yet New England still had an immense pool of experienced and skilled workers. The machinery may have been old and well worn and the mills dirty and stifling, but the region's workers knew how to get the most from the outdated equipment. Workers in older industrial cities used their skills and experience to keep these centers of production going. But it was not a struggle they were ultimately responsible for or capable of winning. At most they could only forestall the inevitable as their wages fell and pressure to produce increased. Mill agents were forced by the divestment of stockholders to compete with newer factories in the South and with new products like rayon.

As textile and shoe centers slipped into decline in New England in the 1920s, newer industries grew. Working with a highly skilled and versatile labor force experienced in building tools and machines for the region's earlier industries, New England entrepreneurs turned to electric motors, machines, and electrical supplies, and to the new radio and tube technology, which gave Raytheon national prominence. The region's extensive hydropower system originally developed for looms, spinners, and carders was refitted in the 1920s to supplement steam-generated electricity. The combination of coastal steam plants and inland hydro plants supplied relatively low uniform electric rates in the region at the very moment when electrification was giving manufacturers an efficiency advantage, especially in those electrochemical and electrometallurgical industries that were heavy electric power consumers. By 1929 there were more than 17,000 workers in the electrical industry in Massachusetts and employment in the electrochemical and electrometallurgical industry was growing. Chicopee's athletic and sporting goods company, A. G. Spalding and Brothers, boomed as the nation embraced the new sporting crazes of tennis and golf.

Although a help to new industry, cheap electricity made little difference to such traditional industries as cotton textiles, where electric power costs were only a small factor in total costs (2 or 3 percent) and labor costs were relatively high. The state's traditional industries still held the largest number of industrial workers: there were more than 62,000 textile workers (a majority of them female), 71,000 shoe workers, 43,000 machine workers producing equipment for the state and nation, more than 18,000 metal workers, and 15,000 rubber workers.[23] Although many hoped that the growth of new industry would cushion the loss of employment in traditional areas, the region's dependence upon older declining industries left many families anxious about the future.

The Great Depression of the 1930s made New England's employment situation worse. Jobs vanished and mills and shops went bankrupt, closed, and were torn down. Workers walked the street without much hope of employment; cities in the Commonwealth went bankrupt; and those industries that were still in operation continued to shave work and cut wages.[24] Unemployment in New England soared into the hundreds of thousands. As late as 1940, there were 206,082 Massachusetts workers still looking for jobs, with regional unemployment reaching almost 400,000, over 11 percent of the work force.[25] In the early years of the Depression, trade unions collapsed and the few workers who had jobs accepted wage cuts as the numbers of desperate unemployed hunting for work grew at the mill gates. With the coming of the New Deal and the passage of the National Industrial Recovery Act with its guarantee of labor's right to unionize (Section 7a), there was a flurry of organizing among New England's traditional labor force: paper workers, textile workers, and shoe workers. In 1934 the region's textile workers joined in the national walkout against wage rates set by the company-dominated NRA Board. The strike ended in defeat for the textile workers, but reactivated unionism in the area. Within three years the leaders of the 1934 strike were building a new union, the Textile Workers Union of America affiliated with the Congress of Industrial Organizations (CIO), which concentrated on organizing unskilled immigrants and their children and the skilled native born of English, Irish, and French Canadian heritage. In the shoe and paper industry, CIO unions organized the unorganized and merged with older unions. The rebirth of unionism was not concentrated among the region's established industries, however. In rubber and electrical industry, New England workers flocked to the CIO, and the machine-tool industry saw a resurgence of the older AFL machinists' union. For all their dynamic energy and dramatic actions, the new unions were only part of the change that swept through New England in the 1930s. The union upsurge came after a long period of divestiture and decline. Unionization was not the cause of decline, only a part of it. Indeed, although some plants may have left New England for the non-union South, the area was gaining jobs in the needle trades as garment shops from New York, in an attempt to escape unionization there, came to locate in empty mills and hire unemployed female textile workers.

Although employment rose slightly during the mid-1930s, unemployment was still the region's and the nation's central problem. Local citizens and governments increasingly looked to the federal government for a solution. For hundreds of New Englanders, employment during the 1930s meant jobs in the New Deal relief programs of the Works Projects Administration, Civilian Works Administration, Public Work Administration, or Civilian Conservation Corps. These programs put people to work on roads, bridges, street lights, schools, libraries, and local histories and murals. As late as 1940, with unemployment in the state over 11 percent, 5.6 percent of the labor force was on some public works project.[26] For government planners, these programs were stop-gap measures that would end with economic recovery. For those employed, these programs represented a new social contract, an implicit promise that if one were willing and able, work would be provided, if not by the private sector then by state or federal government. The New Deal made FDR a popular hero to Massachusetts' working people, and created the expectation of the right to work.

As in other regions, however, it was World War II, not the New Deal, that ended the Depression. Government work relief programs were canceled as workers found jobs making cloth for military uniforms, parachutes, jungle hammocks, army boots, rubber for rain gear, paper for work orders, and machine tools to make machine guns, and the guns and bullets themselves. Full employment returned to the region. Old machines were retooled and repaired, and ancient mills were adapted to the needs of the war effort. New England workers, both men and women, who were skilled, experienced, and proud of their work, enjoyed full employment for the first time in years. New England had a tradition of large numbers of women in the paid labor force which stretched back into the early years of the nineteenth century. "Rosie the war worker" was no newcomer to the New England paid labor force, even if she now worked as a riveter. But although the war returned full employment to New England, it did not alter the fundamental economic landscape.

The New England mills that sprang back to life in the 1940s were very old structures with dated equipment. The war reinvigorated New England's old mills, but it also stimulated the construction of millions of square feet of new factories nationwide and the region did not get its share of new plants. The existent mills and factories of New England discouraged new factory construction, and the national government's attempt to geographically diversify the nation's industry, combined with the underutilized manufacturing capacity of New England, meant that much of the new construction occurred elsewhere. When the war ended, the region's capital stock was solid, but nearly a century old. New single-story factory sites capable of easily incorporating the latest organizational efficiencies built during the war years in other parts of the country now competed with New England's vertically built red brick or stone mills for the new domestic production. Mass-production factory-building technologies that had been developed during the war, as well as profitable tax advantages, greatly reduced the cost of constructing new buildings. The mobility of capital, which had begun to hurt New England in the early years of the twentieth century became even more decisive after the war. Local companies such as A. G. Spalding built new plants outside the region, while other companies were bought out by national corporations that no longer considered local suppliers or local sites when they planned for expansion.[27] Textron, centered in Rhode Island, began buying up textile companies to provide products to the army during the war. With the coming of peace Textron continued buying up local companies, particularly in New England and not only textiles but also machine-tool companies. By the end of the 1940s Textron was selling the assets of its New England companies to finance its diversification outside of textiles and machine tools and into the South. Stockholders in Textron continued to reap benefits as local New England companies were shut down or milked dry.[28]

Although the war experience encouraged greater capital flight by those who controlled the financial assets of the region at war's end, the war workers themselves had not forgotten their New Deal experience. The implicit social contract between the government and those who wanted to work that had emerged during the New Deal was codified in the Employment

Act of 1946 and found expression in the tremendous expansion of public employment in the postwar years. Because the old industries of New England stumbled in the postwar boom, veterans and displaced war workers alike found that there were new jobs in building, repairing, and plowing state and local roads, in school construction, teaching, and administrating, in garbage pick-up and sewer system construction. In the twenty-five years after the war government employment jumped from under 10 percent to close to 20 percent of the civilian work force. These were not the jobs of old: they paid well, had good fringe benefits, and seemed secure in a world of closing mills and factories. As one New England resident said to his son, "you either work for the city, the state, the feds, or you're crazy."[29]

Working for the city, state, or feds did have an entrance fee. That fee was political connection. For those of Irish, English, and French Canadian heritage, generations of community political involvement established the tracks that led into the expanding public jobs. By the 1950s new tracks had been laid to accommodate the children and grandchildren of the Southern and Eastern European immigrants. These were separate tracks, to be sure, and they led into different government jobs. Although New England was not alone in the expansion of public employment, the weakness of its manufacturing base helped fuel the tax revolt which swept Massachusetts in the late 1970s.[30]

Good paying, secure government jobs were not the only jobs growing in New England during the postwar years. New England, like the rest of the nation, also experienced rapid growth in its private-service sector. By 1977 private-service sector jobs—from insurance adjusting and selling, to banking and cleaning hotel rooms—accounted for one-half of New England employment. Many of these jobs in retail and private service paid low wages with few or no benefits.[31]

As the children of those who worked in the mills and factories of the late nineteenth and early twentieth century looked to public employment or services and sales jobs, these children's children spent their youth and young adulthood, not among spinning, weaving, rag sorting, or shredding machines, but in high schools and universities. They were a generation preparing for a different kind of professional work that had been beyond the reach of their parents.

Nevertheless, the old mills continued to employ workers and use machines to make products. Just as the French Canadians and Irish grew used to hearing Italian, Portuguese, Armenian, Polish, and Greek accents among the workers in the early years of the twentieth century, these older workers came to hear Hispanic and African American accents inside the mills in the postwar years. The collapse of the Southern share-cropping system that had taken place with the introduction of new farm technology, particularly the automatic cotton picker and the greater use of tractors and the wide plow on Southern farms, coupled with the continued legacy of racism and violence, led to an upsurge of migrants out of the Southeastern states into the cities of the Northeast in the two decades following the war. During the same period the crisis of subsistence agriculture in the Caribbean, Mexico, and Central America, facilitated by the Green Revolution, led to a huge increase of immigrants, many of them bound for New England. The proportion of African Americans in the region tripled between 1940 and 1960. The number of foreign born from south of the United States' border grew to more than 46,000 by the end of the 1970s, and the number from Spanish origins grew to 141,380 by 1980.[32]

It is this mix of workers that we see in Michael Jacobson-Hardy's pictures. The men and women stand before their machines, as workers would have a hundred years earlier, proud of their manual skills. But notice their machines. These are not the sophisticated computerized devices of the late twentieth century, but rather relics of an industrial past. The buildings are old and jerry-rigged. These are not the settings that will provide employment for a new generation of New Englanders. Fewer and fewer of the region's youth will come to these mills and factories for employment.

For a brief moment in the 1980s, New England seemed to have found an alternative to its mills and factories in the success of its electronics and technical industries. Companies like Raytheon, which had led in developing new technology before the war, helped to fuel an expansion of defense work with the coming of the Cold War. The heavy increase in defense spending in the Reagan years meant a bonanza for "high-tech," expensive war weapons. Defense, plus the initial investment explosion in new computer technology, brought a dramatic renewal to the region's economy. The celebrated high-tech expansion in the computer industry was complemented by the growth of medical technology, which clustered around the region's teaching hospitals and medical centers. The reserve of highly skilled technicians and professionals turned out by the region's densely clustered public and private universities, in an environment of "high" cultural institutions and nature (preserved in part by a half-century of slow growth), made New England ideal for new high-tech start-ups. High wages and benefits in this industry encouraged a new in-migration of other skilled labor, which drove up housing prices and land values. Offices and technology centers, along with new homes and septic systems, day care centers, and nurseries sprang up around the region, and they required labor and materials. The building industry boomed. Workers whose ancestors represented all of the region's past immigrants went to work. With money in their pockets and more members of their family household in the paid labor force, the region's citizens spent more time, and more of the family's budget, eating in new restaurants and fast food establishments. There they were served by the region's children and the newest of the area's immigrants. If we could end the history of New England here, the people of the region would have much to celebrate. Wages seemed to be rising, unemployment dropping, education expanding, and state revenues growing. An empty mill that had given employment to textile, rubber, paper, or machine tool workers might be gutted and refurbished to accommodate some new software supplier or office supply company. Yet even in this positive vision only one in three new jobs in the region was in high tech.[33]

Unfortunately our history does not end in the late 1980s. The high-tech and computer boom did not last. Cuts in defense spending, the shake out of the computer industry, and the outplacing of low-tech computer jobs into low-wage foreign countries brought rapid contraction to the region's economy. As generations of past New Englanders have learned, this generation also is learning the hard lesson that the mobility of capital is greater than the mobility of people. Capital flows to where investment opportunities are greatest, and that often means where labor costs and legislative restrictions are lowest. People, unlike capital, have homes and families. People have ties to a community and networks of support. What encourages capital to look elsewhere for investment—a call for decent wages, union organizing, and rules and regulations governing operations—are the very factors that make a region a better place to live and work. Those factors that appear to threaten profits also encourage a stable and skilled work force, which is in the employers' interest. The tension between wanting a stable, skilled labor force and wanting cheap labor and limited regulations has pulled at New England entrepreneurs and investors for over a hundred years. It has provided space for its workers to struggle for their interests. The dynamics of these struggles can be seen in the ebbs and flows of the New England economy.

New England must once again come to terms with unemployment, falling wages, declining public revenue, and curtailed services. Neither dreaming of the industrial past nor wishing for an expansionist high-tech future makes much sense for New England. Perhaps the best we can do is look into the faces of all our citizens, those in Michael Jacobson-Hardy's pictures, those across the counter in MacDonalds, and those on the street with signs scribbled "work for food" or pushing grocery carts filled with returnable bottles and cans, and ask ourselves, How can this region and this country make their lives as livable as possible?

Notes

1 Lyman Family Papers, vol. 47, Theodore Lyman Papers III, Lyman Scrapbooks, Massachusetts Historical Society, Boston.

2 Lyman Family Papers, vol. 22, Theodore Lyman Papers, Diaries, June 28, 1867.

3 Lyman Family Papers, vol. 47, Lyman Scrapbooks.

4 *Boston Herald,* July 24, 1882.

5 Carroll D. Wright, *Census of Massachusetts, 1885, Populations* (Boston, 1888), 1:529; William Hartford, *Working People of Holyoke: Class and Ethnicity in a Massachusetts Mill Town, 1850–1960* (New Brunswick, N.J.: Rutgers University Press, 1990); 2, 9.

6 Hartford, *Working People,* 49–75; Wright, *Census, 1885,* 1:529.

7 Wright, *Census, 1885,* 1:529.

8 Lyman Diary, June 28, 1867.

9 *Boston Herald,* July 24, 1882.
   See Judith McGaw, *Most Wonderful Machine: Mechanization and Social Change in Berkshire Paper Making, 1801–1885* (Princeton: Princeton University Press, 1987); Thomas Dublin, *Women at Work: The Transformation of Work and Community in Lowell, Massachusetts 1820–1860* (New York: Columbia University Press, 1979); Vera Shlakman, *Economic History of a Factory Town: A Study of Chicopee, Massachusetts,* Smith College Studies in History 20 (1934–1935); Mary Blewett, *Men, Women, and Work: Class, Gender, and Protest in the New England Shoe Industry, 1780–1910* (Champaign-Urbana: University of Illinois Press, 1981); Alan Dawley, *Class and Community: The Industrial Revolution in Lynn* (Cambridge: Harvard University Press, 1976); Paul Faler, *Mechanics and Manufacturers in the Early Industrial Revolution* (Albany: State University of New York Press, 1981); Constance McLaughlin Green, *Holyoke, Massachusetts: A Case History of the Industrial Revolution in America* (New Haven: Yale University Press, 1939); John T. Cumbler, *Working-Class Community in Industrial America: Work, Leisure, and Struggle in Two Industrial Cities, 1880–1930* (Westport, Conn.: Greenwood Press, 1979) for a discussion of worker protest and the development of the early trade union movement in New England.

10 See Dublin, *Women at Work* for a discussion of the makeup of the early textile labor force and the migration patterns of these early factory workers.

11 See Blewett, *Men, Women, and Work* for a discussion of the women in the early shoe shops.

12 See Carolyn Merchant, *Ecological Revolutions: Nature, Gender, and Science in New England* (Chapel Hill: University of North Carolina Press, 1989), especially chaps. 5, 6, 7.

13 Sam Bass Warner and Sylvia Fleisch, *The Measurements for Social History* (Beverly Hills: Sage Publishers, 1977), 137.

14   Ibid.; see also David Ward, *Cities and Immigrants: A Geography of Change in Nineteenth Century America* (New York, Oxford University Press, 1971), 60, 62, 67, 76, 77.

15   See Cumbler, *Working-Class Community*, 105–18, 121–24; Hartford, *Working*, 49–75.

16   See Blewett, *Men, Women, and Work*, 101–90; Cumbler, *Working-Class Community*, 120–25, 158–60, 174.

17   Warner and Fleisch, *Measurements*, 149.

18   Margaret Terrell Parker, *Lowell: A Study of Industrial Development* (Port Washington: Kennikat Press, 1970), 201.

19   Cumbler, *Working-Class Community*, 89.

20   President's Commission on Unemployment, Herbert Hoover, chair, *Recent Economic Trends* (New York: McGraw-Hill, 1929), 934.

21   Abraham Berglund, George Starnes, and Frank de Vyver, *Labor in the Industrial South* (Charlottesville: University of Virginia Institute for Research in the Social Sciences, 1930), 72–99.

22   Alex Keyssar, *Out of Work* (Cambridge: Cambridge University Press, 1986), Table A.5, 320–24.

23   U.S. Bureau of Census, *Fifteenth Census of the United States: 1930, Occupations*, 4:691, 692, 693. See also Parker, *Lowell*, 160.

24   Cumbler, *Working-Class Community*, 89, 90, 139–43.

25   U.S. Bureau of Census, *Sixteenth Census of the United States: 1940, Population*, 3:27.

26   Ibid.

27   See Barry Bluestone and Bennett Harrison, *The Deindustrialization of America: Plant Closings, Community Abandonment, and the Dismantling of Basic Industry* (New York: Basic Books 1982), 25–48; Larry Sawers and William Tabb, *Sunbelt/Snowbelt: Urban Development and Regional Restructuring* (New York: Oxford University Press, 1984) for a discussion of the process of deindustrialization in New England.

28   Bluestone and Harrison, *Deindustrialization*, 124, 182–83, Appendix A-5.

29   Ronald Helberg's father's comment to his adult son after the bakery factory Ronald worked in closed in the early 1970s. Overheard by author.

     For national figures on public service employment see Stanley Lebergott, *Manpower in Economic Growth: The American Record since 1800* (New York: McGraw-Hill, 1964), 514, 517.

30   John T. Cumbler, *A Social History of Economic Decline* (New Brunswick, N.J.: Rutgers University Press, 1989), 145–47, 167–75; Hartford, *Working*, chap. 8.

31   Bluestone and Harrison, *Deindustrialization*, 95.

32   Warner and Fleisch, *Measurements* 175, 192. U.S. Bureau of Census *Twentieth Census of the United States: 1980*, 1, pt. 23, secs. 2, 7.

33   Bluestone and Harrison, *Deindustrialization*, 95.

Objectivities and Subjectivities:
The Ambiguities of Documentary Photography

ROBERT E. WEIR

Michael Jacobson-Hardy's photographs of factories, work, and laborers are part of the social documentary tradition of American photography. Some of his compositions are striking and beautiful, others are disturbing in their social implications. Like much documentary photography, Jacobson-Hardy's work blurs the boundaries between art and politics; his images are at once striking compositions, but at the same time calls for social justice. Documentary photography appears under various labels, including social photography, photo essay, reform photography, social landscape photography, and photo story, but whatever it is called, most of it pretends to replicate the clarity and purity espoused by Francis Bacon;[1] indeed, his quote graced the darkroom door of Dorothea Lange, one of America's greatest social documentarians. As Susan Sontag reminds us, however, such goals are simplistic and naive.[2]

In truth, the tradition to which Jacobson-Hardy belongs is a complex one whose motives, meanings, and uses have changed and continue to evolve. One commentator grappling for a way to capture these shifting meanings concluded that documentary photography was either "just about everything" or "just about nothing." Though one might disagree with such a pessimistic assessment, the confrontational nature of social documentary photography often makes its messages matters for debate. As Jacobson-Hardy puts it, "I am pushing the edges of what we allow ourselves to look at."[3] By doing so, he raises awareness and ire.

Much of the frustration in making sense of documentary photographs comes from a desire to order and label intertwined phenomena as though they were discrete. Sontag's observations remind us that the social uses of photography inevitably meld with the aesthetics of art. But as I have already suggested, art is not the only force that shapes the documentary impulse. This essay will examine the dialectical relationships between the form of documentary photography and its various contexts. It proceeds from the assumption that there is no clear line that divides the objective and the subjective; that is, Michael Jacobson-Hardy's photographs are a pastiche of facts and visions—at once, representations of objective historical reality and products of subjective political and artistic inputs.

The Historical Sweep of Documentary Photography

For its part, photography dates from 1839 when it was announced that Louis Daguerre had captured images on chemically treated metal plates.[4] By the spring of that same year, the Frenchman's sensational experiments spawned worldwide imitations, including several in the United States. Novelty dominated the first days of image-making as the public mobbed galleries and rival technologies vied for supremacy. Portraits, collages, and illusions wowed audiences, but the bulk of early photographs often appeared as little more than pictorial versions of court documents, and their surfaces suggest few intrusions of ideology. Not until the 1850s was it clear that fad would give way to industry and craft. This change was represented by the widespread use of the term "photography," a word coined in 1839 but largely dormant until the 1850s. It supplanted labels associated with specific inventors and heralded the universality of the art form.[5] Nonetheless, early equipment was temperamental and chemicals unpredictable and unstable, so much so that well into the 1870s many critics and practitioners saw a "photographer" as the person who coaxed forth the image in the darkroom, whereas the camera's manipulator was a mere "operator."

Part of the problem in determining what documentary photography is and does, is that the term "documentary" is elusive and shifting. Although nineteenth-century photographers and commentators sometimes called images "documents," as often as not their references owed more to legalistic notions of what constituted an "official" record than to matters for public policy debate. Documentary did not assume its modern connotations until after 1926 when British movie director John Grierson first used the term to refer to films whose purpose was primarily cultural, didactic, and scientific rather than commercial or escapist. By appropriating a term hitherto confined mostly to logic and law, Grierson opened the door for others to explore the interstices between record keeping, artistic expression, and social policy. Even then, it would not be until the Great Depression that most photographers working in the genre described their work as "documentary" expression.[6]

Although there were harbingers of documentary expression, it was the Civil War that brought it to the fore in the United States. For example, the most important collection of early topical work were the daguerreotypes of Richard Beard that illustrated Henry Mayhew's *London Labour and the London Poor* (1855). American photographers, however, were little affected by Beard's work because it was reproduced for publication as woodcuts. In the United States, it was Matthew Brady who made photography something more than a novel alternative to portrait and landscape painting. Although Brady was seldom the "operator" behind the camera and his was one of several rival studios to produce images of the Civil War, he got the lion's share of the credit for chronicling America's greatest internal tragedy. (He got little else. Brady's successful portrait gallery faltered after the Civil War and he sold much of his famed war collection to pay off debts. He died a pauper in 1896.)

Brady's work was path breaking in the way that his images implied meaning beyond the mere capture of moments frozen in time. His was the simple but straightforward message that war is horrific. By leaving political justifications for conflict aside, Brady emphasized the human dimension of war. The first images to cause a stir were those made for Brady in 1862 by Alexander Gardner following the Battle of Antietam. Gardner's images of corpses strewn by fences—some of which had been moved to create stronger composition—and dead soldiers bloating in the fields with the moment of death fixed on their faces evoked horror among the throngs who passed through Brady's New York City studio. These techniques were repeated at Gettysburg and other battle sites. Brady admitted that he wished to convince the masses that war was barbaric so that future violence could be averted.[7] But his images demonstrate clearly the ways in which the photographer's vision can be subverted by audience readings. Crowds were shocked to be sure, but they were also angered. Northern audiences mixed the strong Brady images with other visual stimuli: illustrated newspapers, magic lantern shows depicting battles, more sensational photos made by Gardner after his split with Brady, picture cards hawked on the streets, and images of Federal prisoners in Southern prisoner of war camps. Much to his chagrin, Brady's photographs incensed the Northern public. In a way, the Brady photos were a sort of visual *Uncle Tom's Cabin*. Many Northerners had already been convinced of their moral superiority through the efforts of abolitionists and champions of free labor ideology.[8] In effect, instead of softening attitudes, Brady's photos helped convert Northerners to new ideas of "total war" championed by Ulysses S. Grant and William Tecumseh Sherman. It was claimed that the ferocity with which Sherman's troops marched across Georgia was inflamed by photos purporting to show Southern atrocities. Brady's intentions were further subverted by antiquarians and historians who treated him as a mere chronicler capturing the Civil War for future generations.[9]

The photographers of Brady's generation opened themselves to such reinterpretation by hiding their subjectivity behind a veil of factual objectivity. One of the first to stress openly his subjectivity was Danish-born Jacob Riis whose collected photos and comments for various newspapers and magazines were published in book form in 1890. That work, *How the Other Half Lives*, earned Riis the title "Emancipator of the Slums." Working as a police reporter, Riis was a frequent observer of the squalor and degradation of New York City's Lower East Side. His images first circulated as woodcuts, but during the 1890s, improvements in the half-tone process allowed newspapers to reproduce photos more cheaply and clearly. This innovation thrust Riis's images to the fore of the effort to improve the lot of New York City slum dwellers. One New Yorker moved by Riis's work was its new police commissioner, Theodore Roosevelt, who closed some of the East Side's ruder boardinghouses. Riis was also evoked in 1901, when the state's tenement house laws were rewritten.[10]

For all of that, Riis, by his own admission as well as the judgment of art critics, was not a particularly gifted photographer. There is a relentless sameness to his photos, as well as a great degree of clutter that weakens overall composition. In addition, most of Riis's human subjects looked away from the camera. The averted glance deadened and dehumanized his subjects, a technique that was in keeping with Riis's own Anglocentrism. Although sympathetic to the plight of the poor, Riis retained a sense of Victorian morality and accepted without question prevailing assumptions of Aryan superiority.[11]

The first American to bridge the gap between documentary-as-exposé and documentary-as-art was Lewis Hine. Of his reform instincts Hine made no bones: "I wanted to show the things that had to be corrected." But in the next breath, Hine embedded an artistic aesthetic: "I wanted to show the things that had to be appreciated."[12] Hine's work as a reformer and artist are still underrated; even one of his scholarly admirers claims that "Hine cannot be seen historically except in light of his reception and belated acceptance in the 1930s," and then only through "the light of Alfred Stieglitz," whose emphasis on the artfulness of photography eventually influenced Hine.[13]

The latter claim is true if financial success and public acclaim are the measuring sticks, but Hine's reformist zeal pushed such considerations to the background in the early part of his career. Hine surfaced as the Progressive Era dawned. He turned to photography in 1903, after brief stints as a student at the University of Chicago and then as a teacher in New York City's Ethical Culture School. His first images were of immigrants passing through Ellis Island. Unlike most documentary photographers, Hine was a reformer for the greater part of his career. Immigrants, laborers, work, and working conditions made the bulk of his collected work; his commercial images are undistinguished and few. His intense moralism and reformist zeal led him to Progressive groups that needed and respected his work, but they seldom paid well. From 1906 through 1917, the cause of child labor most animated Hine. As a freelancer for the National Child Labor Committee (NCLC) and as a staff photographer for *The Survey* and for *Charities and the Common*, Hine traveled across the country to document the horrors of child labor at a time when some two million children under the age of sixteen spent their days in toil rather than in schools. He often developed elaborate ruses to get into factories and was in physical jeopardy on more than one occasion when employers discovered his true identity and purpose. In the face of adversity and resistance, Hine proved remarkably successful; his strong 1910 images made in Buffalo, New York, Illinois, and Alabama raised thousands of dollars in NCLC donations.

In addition to his child labor photos, Hine continued documenting immigrants through the 1920s. During World War I, he went to Europe and made more than four hundred images for the American Red Cross. His shots of Belgian refugees in particular raised public sympathy and spurred donations for relief efforts.

Even now Hine's pre-1930 photos evoke powerful emotions; many have become instantly recognizable historical icons, like his shots of subteen breaker boys astride coal chutes in Pennsylvania and those of stocking knitters in Southern mills in which the youngest pig-tailed girls stand on boxes to reach their machines. One also sees in these photos the strong composition and contrasts that make Hine's work distinctive. A 1910 shot of a New York City beggar juxtaposes the man's sunken eyes and unshaven face against the backdrop of a razor advertisement emblazoned with the word "Beautiful."

Hine fell on hard financial times by the late 1920s. His early work was very much part and parcel of Progressive Era reform. Hine was no radical; as Alan Trachtenberg put it, his work was "critical of social and economic injustices in view of conventional American values of common sense and fair play." Thus he looked "to collective rather than individual solutions—to legislative and corporate forms of recognizing the industrial order to diminish conflicts."[14] But such faith in American institutions was misplaced in the 1920s, and both Hine and his causes languished by the decade's end.

The construction of the Empire State Building in 1930 moved Hine to new interpretive heights. Many of these photos made their way into a 1932 book, *Men at Work*, and likewise achieved iconic status. His most famous image is of a young man astride a swaying cable a quarter mile above the New York City skyline. Some commentators have misinterpreted *Men at Work* as a move away from social criticism, but such a view misses the subtlety of these photos.[15] In Hine's own words, these photos were a very important offset to some misconceptions about industry . . . one is that our material assets "just happen" as the product of a bunch of impersonal machines, under the direction . . . of a few human robots. . . . It is for the sake of emphasis, not exaggeration, that I select the more pictorial personalities . . . for it is the only way that I can illustrate my thesis that the human spirit is the big thing after all.[16]

These photos and his *Through the Loom* portfolio displayed at the 1933 New York World's Fair were among the last that garnered steady income for Lewis Hine. Ironically, he had trouble getting regular work during the Depression, the golden age of American documentary expression. He took some photos for the Tennessee Valley Authority and a few for New Deal agencies such as the Works Progress Administration (including an unfinished project in Holyoke, Massachusetts) and the Civilian Conservation Corps, but not enough to stave off financial ruin. He was twice turned down for Guggenheim grants and landed very little work from Roy Stryker, the head of the Farm Security Administration's Historical Division. Hine was bankrupt by the time that art critic Elizabeth McCausland and photographer Berenice Abbott organized a 1939 retrospective of his work for New York's Riverside Museum. He enjoyed brief celebrity, but little gain before his death in 1940.[17]

Although like Brady, Hine died in poverty, he was destined to have far more impact on the genre of documentary photography. Unlike Riis, Hine had genuine compassion for subjects that nervous Victorians would have labeled as debased, degraded, and dangerous. He imbued his subjects with humanity and left little doubt that their plight was due to social conditions rather than moral failings or character flaws. The crusading impulses unleashed by Hine came to full flower in the 1930s. As Hine worked in vain for reform in the 1920s, a younger generation of photographers honed their skills in other ways. Margaret Bourke-White made a comfortable living in industrial photography; Dorothea Lange, as a commercial photographer; and John Collier, Jr., Jack Delano, and Ben Shahn, as painters; Berenice Abbott and Walker Evans tramped across Europe sharpening their skills in photography and social criticism. The Great Depression awakened the social consciousness of each of them, and many began attending events sponsored by the Photo League, an organization formed in 1928 with links to the Communist Party. The League was set up to record events like strikes and demonstrations unreported in the mainstream press.[18] By sponsoring lectures, classes, and workshops, it also trained an entire generation of social documentarians before its demise in 1947. Much of their work was published in its *Photo Notes* newsletter. (As a recruiting tool, it was weak; very few of the photographers involved with the Photo League ever joined the Communist Party.)

A list of American photographers working in the social documentary genre during the 1930s reads like a photographic hall of fame: Berenice Abbott, Margaret Bourke-White, Robert Capa, John Collier, Jr., Jack Delano, Eliot Eliosfan, Walker Evans, Dorothea Lange, Russell Lee, Arthur Rothstein, Ben Shahn, Paul Strand, and John Vachon. There were a host of others. Even photographers associated with the formal and abstract principles espoused by the influential Group f/64 occasionally turned their gaze to documentary expression. (Ansel Adams was one of the few holdouts who refused to document "political economy with emotion. . . .")[19] Their work was aided by technological advances such as the perfection of flash bulbs, by the proliferation of small hand-held cameras, and by the emergence of photo magazines like *Life* (1936) and *Look* (1937), themselves products of the new photographic technology.[20]

The Depression and Photo League stirred the social consciousness of many photographers, technological change improved their craft, and the media helped popularize their work. But it was the New Deal that put photographers to work and elevated documentary expression to respectability. From 1935 through 1941, the Farm Security Administration and its predecessor, the Resettlement Administration, collected some 270,000 photographs. Although much of this work was destined for archival files, a substantial amount made its way to the public eye; 175 magazines used FSA images between 1938 and 1940.[21] Many photographers found the FSA's Roy Stryker temperamental and, on occasion, a poor arbiter of taste, but few could deny his role in advancing awareness of documentary expression. Stryker helped organize the First International Exposition of Photography, which opened in New York City in April 1938 to critical acclaim and large crowds. Walker Evans simultaneously held his first Museum of Modern Art show. Before 1938, the term "documentary photography" was not yet in wide currency; by year's end, even Edward Steichen was forced to admit that it was "all the rage."[22] By 1939, critics and the public at large argued over its proper use.[23] By the end of the decade, the documentary impulse dominated all American artistic expression.[24]

The debate over documentary content raged (and still rages) with an intensity flamed, in no small part, by the differing styles, objectives, and opinions of photographers themselves. Professional jealousy also reared its head, especially in the criticisms heaped upon Margaret Bourke-White whose 1937 photo-textual collaboration with Erskine Caldwell, *You Have Seen Their Faces,* was a commercial success. Bourke-White wrote captions for her photos, anathema to contemporaries such as Lange and Evans, who accused her of putting words in her subjects' mouths. They were equally put off by Bourke-White's carefully posed compositions.[25] Nonetheless, she stimulated others to try their hand at publication. In 1938, the poet Archibald MacLeish published *Land of the Free*, a rambling reflection of the American social landscape illustrated with photos from FSA and Associated Press files. The next year, Lange and Paul Taylor issued *An American Exodus: A Record of Human Erosion*, a photo essay of the Dust Bowl. Walker Evans published two books, *American Photographs* in 1938 and *Let Us Now Praise Famous Men*, his 1941 collaboration with writer James Agee. Evans complained that Bourke-White's work was deceptive and his more pure, but his books—although they met with critical acclaim—were ignored by the general public.

In recent years, the FSA material has come under as much scrutiny as that of Bourke-White. Research and textual analysis has revealed that few Depression-era photographers contemplated "things as they are without substitution or imposture," and that Lange and Evans were as guilty of this deception as anyone. The FSA photographs exhibit what one critic calls a "doctrinal aspect" in that they deal with "worthy" subjects, all of whom could be comfortably seen as "victims" of the Depression, rather than being hoboes, addicts, derelicts, or others whose narratives were more problematic.[26] In essence, many photographers flirted with socialist realism, an expressive form driven more by ideological assumptions than by a search for balance or representativeness. Even Roy Stryker admitted that he "edited" FSA files. Since the FSA retained ownership of negatives, it was easy for Stryker to crop images and to adapt individual shots for whatever purpose he deemed necessary.[27]

Both the Depression and the FSA ended with America's preparation for World War II. The war redefined the nature of documentary content and rendered debate over its political biases moot; most art became openly propagandistic in its support of American war efforts. In essence, Joe Rosenthal's famous shot of GIs raising the flag on Iwo Jima typified World War II documentary photography. War-time photos captured Americans in combat, but with an emphasis on the heroic. Notably absent were images of American dead like those of Matthew Brady eighty years earlier. When *Life* magazine printed George Strock's photos of

Americans killed in New Guinea, the public outrage was so great that in the future, censors excised such images.[28] When dead or dying were shown, the images served to reinforce perceptions of allied progress—as in shots of German and Japanese casualties—or to reinforce justifications for sacrifice, as in the horrific images of Nazi concentration camp victims.

In the postwar era, photographers tended to be more introspective in their approach to documentary expression. Several late Photo League students, such as Jerome Liebling, Ruth Orkin, and Aaron Siskind, produced remarkable work that garnered critical raves, but stripped of government sponsorship and facing a public more interested in postwar industrial conversion and the Cold War, documentary photographers found their work to be weak reform stimuli. More important, sympathy for the working class, the chief subject of the past, simply fell from fashion. Would-be documentarians turned in increasing numbers to the mass media where they found more restrictions and less concern for social justice than existed in New Deal agencies. In short, photography lost the unifying focus provided by government orchestration of Depression images.

As commentators like Henry Luce touted the opening of the "American Century," the social and political stresses and divisions of the 1930s yielded to searches for consensus and pressure for conformity. Not surprisingly, photography in the 1950s was more particularistic, less critical, and more distant than that of the 1930s. Documentary expression yielded to the "photo essay," often an illustrated news story and usually marked by uniqueness rather than universality. *Life* printed Margaret Bourke-White's remarkable photos from India in the late 1940s, and her equally brilliant shots of South African gold miners in 1950, but they failed to stir imaginations like those she had taken of Southern poor in the 1930s. Several projects were stunning, including W. Eugene Smith's 1951 *Life* photo essay of an African American midwife in the rural South and Gordon Parks's on-going series of a Brazilian peasant boy which he started in 1961. But as Abigail Solomon-Godeau notes, devoid of directed ideological underpinnings, exposés easily transmute into "exoticism, tourism, voyeurism, psychologism . . . trophy hunting and careerism."[29] Many of those elements are preserved in the Museum of Modern Art's catalog of the decade's most famous photo exhibition, "The Family of Man" show organized by Edward Steichen in 1955.[30]

The dawning of the television age further eroded the central role of documentary photography. Some well-known photos were mere stills of moving images such as Matthew Zimmerman's picture of Marilyn Monroe's billowing skirt, arguably the single most famous image of the 1950s. Also troublesome was the renewed respectability of nonrepresentational art that blossomed in the 1950s, a phenomenon that reinvigorated experimental and abstract photography. Those photographers who sought the social critic's mantle often turned to a documentary spinoff dubbed "social landscape photography," which tended to concentrate on the fragmented and anomic qualities of urban life. Robert Frank and Lee Friedlander were central to this subgenre. Still others, like Diane Arbus, sought to evoke moods through the use of harsh lighting and odd angles, effective techniques that pushed further the debate over how "real" was the documentarian world.[31]

The social turmoil of the 1960s proved a temporary boon for documentary photography. The civil rights movement produced such memorable images as those of impeccably dressed young African American students being harassed by angry whites at a Greensboro lunch counter and those taken by Charles Moore of attack dogs tearing at civil rights demonstrators in Birmingham. The Vietnam conflict produced numerous memorable images: Malcolm Browne's shot of a Buddhist monk's self-immolation, Eddie Adams's chilling picture of an on-the-spot execution of a suspected Vietcong terrorist, Ron Haeberle's My Lai massacre documentation, and Huynh Cong Ut's pathos-laden image of a burnt, screaming, naked girl fleeing a napalm attack.[32] These frozen images were, in truth, much bolder and more critical of American behavior than most television images which, until 1968, seldom showed American troops or their South Vietnamese allies in a negative light.[33]

In addition, countercultural lifestyles also attracted camera attention. *Life*'s images of the 1969 Woodstock music festival proved so popular that the Time-Life Corporation printed a special collection of festival photos that sold millions of copies. Student protests were captured by the camera's lens as well, and two images stand out: John Paul Filo's shot of anguished fourteen-year-old Mary Ann Vecchio kneeling over a slain Kent State student and Bernie Boston's photo of an antiwar protestor inserting a flower into a national guardsman's rifle. Both are standard fare in books on recent American history.

Nevertheless, not even the upheaval of civil rights, Vietnam, the counterculture, and student protest returned documentary photography to its glory days of the 1930s. By 1970, Eugene Smith complained (perhaps naively) that his work was a failure as it had not contributed to ending warfare, injustice, and suffering.[34] (Nonetheless, Smith went on documenting these things and in 1971 produced a chilling series on the effects of mercury poisoning on Japanese villagers from Minamata.) In the 1970s, color photography—spurred in no little part by the emergence of Polaroid cameras—supplanted black and white in public preference. Color reproduction is more expensive; one victim of this was the photo news magazine. The demise of weeklies like *The Saturday Evening Post*, *Life*, and *Look* further eroded the outlets for social documentarians.

But more than anything else, these magazines were done in by the electronic media. Television became ubiquitous in the 1950s and dominant in the 1960s. Since 1963, an increasingly larger majority of Americans get their news from television rather than newspapers or magazines. By 1977, only 42 percent of the American public relied on the print media for information. Among the few commercial outlets for documentary photographs these days are newspapers and news magazines, and even their numbers are dwindling.[35] New concern for the future of documentary photography is raised by the specter of savvy media image-makers who carefully construct "photo opportunities" and plot strategies for "managing" the news by keeping troublesome photographers (and news reporters) out of situations in which they might have a chance to reveal other than the "official" line. Consider, for example, the way in which the Bush administration and the U.S. military banned reporters from the early stages of both Operation Desert Storm in Iraq and Operation Restore Hope in Somalia. Those reporters and photographers who fail to play by the rules—like CNN's Peter Arnett who stayed in Baghdad—must endure withering attacks on their professional judgment, personal character, and patriotism.

Small wonder then that many documentarians since the 1970s have turned inward toward what some have called "recording the private world," investigations into ambience, emotion, and mood rather than social conditions.[36] Like Americans from all walks of life, many photographers grew to distrust politics and institutions. But this does not mean that documentary photography has little future or that the photos of Michael Jacobson-Hardy are an anachronistic throwback. For one thing, photos slow down the viewer in the age of television, which is important in a culture that has seen the average television "sound bite" decline from nearly forty-six seconds in the early 1960s to fewer than ten seconds by the 1980s. Psychologically, a single image is more likely to stimulate a viewer's emotions than the rapidly changing montage of moving images. As Susan Sontag notes, "The camera is the ideal arm of consciousness in its acquisitive mood."[37] Consider, for example, several frozen images from the 1960s: John F. Kennedy at the moment he was struck by the assassin's bullet, his brother Robert lying in a pool of blood in Los Angeles, and the discharge of Jack Ruby's gun into the stomach of Lee Harvey Oswald. Each image is more powerful, chilling, and evocative than the videos taken at the same time because each forces us to linger in detailed and sustained horror rather than escaping psychologically into the confusion, clutter, and motion of the videos. More recently, millions of dollars pored into relief agencies after *Newsweek* and *Time* printed heart-wrenching images of starvation victims in Chad, Ethiopia, and Sudan.

Frozen images do more than engage emotions; they also allow for reflection and intellectual investigation. Photographer Jim Hubbard has raised awareness concerning the homeless in a series of chilling portraits. He also taught children to use the camera and allowed them to document the challenges of life among the underclass in his *Shooting Back* photo essay. In a project with parallels to Michael Jacobson-Hardy's work, photographer Milton Rogovin forces viewers to consider the human costs of closed steel mills in Buffalo, New York.[38]

But one does not have to be a social critic to appreciate the importance of careful contemplation. Indeed, as one commentator notes, "most people see more accurately when examining a photograph of an object than when observing the object itself."[39] Jacobson-Hardy's photos make plenty of statements that have little to do with one's political persuasions. When we pause to take in detail, we become open to multiple messages and deeper understanding. Jacobson-Hardy's images raise important questions about social and industrial policy, but they also speak to other human dimensions such as pride, resiliency, and the dignity of labor. In addition, we admire aesthetic considerations such as composition, form, and line.

Two other qualities offered by good documentary photography concern the way it orders reality and the manner in which it preserves the past. The first function is of particular importance in a society dazzled by such speed and change as to make thorough comprehension of any given phenomenon difficult. Photographers in the 1930s humanized economic events and thus helped Americans better understand the Depression. They took it upon themselves to record tragedy for the sake of posterity.[40] Jacobson-Hardy's photographs reveal much about the changing nature of work, the human drama that unfolds in the workplace, and the human dimensions of deindustrialization, mechanization, and a changing economy. In the present, his photos are "evidence" for debates over social policy; at some point in the future, they will help Americans make sense of public policy.

Above all, Jacobson-Hardy adds real human faces to abstract discussions about economic and social policy. Like Lewis Hine, Jacobson-Hardy emphasizes machines and workplaces and contextualizes them by adding workers. His shot of lint-covered José Cumba, for example, personalizes work in a paper mill more effectively than words. But his work is also preservationist. Much of it evokes Hine because many of the factories and work patterns he documents are antiquated and soon to disappear. But they also show how much has survived, suggest what is to come, and raise larger questions about the nature of work in our society. (Is the protective eye wear of the iron foundry worker all that different from the special glasses worn by computer line workers?) Like Hine, Jacobson-Hardy can be said to produce "the Human Document to keep the present and future in touch with the past."[41]

Documentary or Propaganda?

As in the case of Lewis Hine, there will be those who will look at Michael Jacobson-Hardy's photographs and dismiss them as biased. In fact, one cannot dodge the charge that all documentary expression is essentially an act of opinion.[42] Any act of persuasion is potentially a subjective political act. For photographers, bias emerges in the choice of subjects, the way they are presented, and the centrality accorded them. But it would be a mistake to pretend that artistic constructions are mere opinions ungrounded in objective reality.

What we call "history" consists of both an actual event and a series of constructed interpretations conditioned by cultural, political, and social preferences. Likewise, every photo that captures objective reality is also a product of the photographer's worldview because the image shows both what *is* there and what *ought* to be there. For Hine or Lange, each of their images was also a commentary on injustice. One observer calls this the "melioristic" impulse in which a certain degree of "slanting" is necessary in order to get a message across.[43] All documentary photographers seek to stimulate both the intellect and the emotions.[44] For that second reason, Depression-era photographers found women and children to be good subjects; the public perceived them to be more vulnerable.

In retrospect, it is easy to exaggerate the intellectual motives of the photographers of the

1930s. Many historians and critics have given belated praise to Walker Evans, assumed to be the most "objective" of all chroniclers of the Depression. Yet, as several studies reveal, Evans routinely rearranged objects, posed his subjects, and ignored details that conflicted with the look he hoped to achieve. Many of the era's most famous images can be said to have been "faked" if one wishes to hold photographers to Bacon's dictum. Arthur Rothstein moved a bleached steer skull he found in South Dakota in order to make it appear that the animal was the victim of drought. He also labeled another photo "Fleeing a Dust Storm" when other shots taken of the same man and his son clearly show that there was no dust storm that day. Even Dorothea Lange's "Migrant Mother," perhaps the most renowned picture in American photographic history, was her fifth image; it was cropped in the darkroom and was probably posed.[45] But knowing all this, it remains ahistorical to deny the existence of the Dust Bowl or Depression-era despair.

Nonetheless, historians and photographers alike must grapple with those who would look for ways to deny the subject through exposure of intent. In 1937, Charles Beard, Paul Douglas, and Robert Lynd founded the Institute for Propaganda Analysis to help expose media and image bias. As we have seen, Margaret Bourke-White came under fire for writing photo captions. More recently, *Matewan,* a John Sayles film about a West Virginia coal strike in 1920, was attacked as anticapitalist propaganda. Several reviewers delighted in showing that Sayles invented characters, telescoped events, and added fanciful details for which there were no records.[46] One might just as easily expose the ideologies of the critics, but such an exercise detracts from more important questions. Can a work be both subjective and true? Is all fiction entirely false? Must we learn everything in order to know anything?

It is often more comfortable to attack a work as propaganda than to deal with its messages. Documentary photographers can act as the superego to the social id and expose the cruelty, greed, injustice, and ugliness that undergirds social systems. To dismiss something as "mere" opinion implies that somehow "real" society is less subjective than the photographer's vision of it. In truth, society is a system of power relationships consciously constructed. When a photographer like Michael Jacobson-Hardy presents us with images of ugly abandoned factories or demeaning images of work, those buildings and jobs are not the only ones in town. But neither are they isolated aberrations. As Bourke-White observed, a single image can lie, "but a group of pictures can't."[47] Jacobson-Hardy documents deindustrialization in New England, but how many Holyokes could a team of like-minded photographers unearth if they traversed America?

Some photographers have been forthcoming in their intent to reform. Lewis Hine identified himself as "social agitator first and photographer second."[48] He entitled a 1909 speech "Social Photography: How the Camera May Help Social Uplift." When his child labor photos spawned cries of deception Hine countered that they "set the authorities to work to see 'if such things can be possible.' They try to get around them by crying 'Fake,' but therein lies the value of the data and a witness."[49] Most documentarians, from Hine to the present, hope to achieve social change. Many projects, like this one, have resorted to combining photographs and text in order to reinforce their visions.

Those who feel uncomfortable with subjective truth can take solace in the way one group of subjectivities is affected by others. Hine began to integrate text with his photos when he learned that the *International Socialist Review* was using his photos as a call to insurrection. As a Progressive reformer, Hine retained faith in the ability of existing institutions to resolve social problems. The man who viewed himself as a reformer with a camera had little sympathy with those who called for revolution. Likewise, Walker Evans complained, "People often read things into my work, but I did not consciously put these things in the photographs."[50] It is easy to be led astray by the subject matter of Evans's Depression-era work and to assign to him ideological assumptions he did not hold. Evans's eye for composition was far better developed than his understanding of the political economy. Moreover, his primary artistic interest was in folk architecture, not social problems. Those who would label him a radical reformer ignore the fact that he was an associate editor of *Fortune* magazine from 1945 to 1965 and a graphic design professor at Yale from 1965 until his death ten years later.

Even the best documentary record is usually an incomplete analysis of any phenomenon. As Curtis puts it, "a photograph has no inherent or intrinsic message—only an assigned meaning."[51] For all their lip service to "objective" truth, many documentary photographers have been left of center and have viewed their craft as a sort of bully pulpit from which they can inform and convert their audiences to the cause of social reform. But, as Curtis reminds us, skill in manipulating images is no guarantee that the public will derive the meaning the photographer intended. As often as not, sweeping change does not result from photographers' work. It can even be argued that the documentary photographs frequently have unintended conservative impulses. The photographer may have strong political views, but how does one convey one's politics? In images of labor, one can represent workers and conditions, perhaps even evoke pathos, but how does one show the effects of international trade? Capital flight? Technological change? Business unionism? Political trade-off? Good documentary helps us humanize and personalize to the point that we empathize with Eleanor, José, or Ray, but we are left with an incomplete understanding of historical forces.

Documentary photography is a complicated interplay involving the photographer's intent and the audience that views the images. Ideology, aesthetics, and time mediate and ensure that the meaning of any image is more subjective than ultimate. But this does not destroy what is "objective" about images. We can, if we so chose, dismiss Michael Jacobson-Hardy's photographs as artful manipulations. We cannot, however, so easily dispense with the objective reality of deindustrialization. John Cumbler's essay documents this thoroughly. In addition, one need go no further than the local paper for more examples. Since the 1960s, the city of Pittsfield, Massachusetts, has seen employment at its local General Electric plant drop from 11,000 to its current level of 3,150 and more than 2,000 of those existing jobs are jeopardized by GE's recent decision to sell its aerospace division.[52] Just an hour east, three Massachusetts counties saw manufacturing jobs decrease from 58,730 to 50,100 between 1988 and 1991, a decline of nearly 19 percent.[53] Statewide, Massachusetts has lost some 400,000 jobs in the same period. In southern New Hampshire, Portsmouth citizens contemplate a future with an aging shipyard that in the past two years has shed more than 9,000 of its work force of 15,400 and that may close altogether.[54]

Jacobson-Hardy has indeed captured a "real" phenomenon no matter what subjective biases exist behind the viewfinder. He has recorded work patterns destined for historical and sociological study. What it all means is uncertain at best. John Cumbler has projected some trends and has offered a few visions of what the future might look like. His are informed opinions, but they too are subjective viewpoints. So too are those emotions, thoughts, and analyses stimulated in those individuals gazing at Jacobson-Hardy's photographs. But let us not relinquish our responsibility to be analytical and informed in the vain notion that all is "mere" opinion. It is only through the welter of emotion, opinion, facts, and subjectivity that we understand our past, order our present, and project our future.

But Is It Art?

Of the thousands of images taken during the Depression, why do we remember "Migrant Mother" and a handful of others above all the rest? Why do museums hold Lewis Hine retrospectives fifty years after his death? Why do historians and critics rave over shots taken by Walker Evans, which the public ignored in their own day? Why publish this book? Much of the discussion thus far has addressed the social and historical value of documentary photographs, but another reason to look at them is that they are works of art imbued with intrinsic worth; in short, art for art's sake. If all photographic meaning is assigned, then the entire debate over objectivity and truthfulness is moot. The message of a photograph changes over time, but a strong composition remains striking for as long as the image survives.

The much ballyhooed debate between Lewis Hine and Alfred Stieglitz over the purpose of photography is assumed to have split the craft into "use" versus "art" camps, divisions made permanent during the Depression and embodied in the differences between works produced by the FSA and those of Group f/64. But as photographers and historians are both fond of saying, "there's more to this than meets the eye." We have seen that a substantial number of documentary photographers came to the craft via a fine arts background. As one commentator notes, this is because both painting and photography are "full of interpretation" and walk the thin line between "truth and art." Why did Arthur Rothstein move the steer skull or Walker Evans rearrange furniture? Why did Dorothea Lange remove an intrusive thumb from her final print of "Migrant Mother"? Simply because their embellishments made stronger compositions. In David Peeler's words, "With an impressive kit bag of techniques, Rothstein and the others could stage their subjects, catch them in candid moments, and provoke their emotions."[55] The point is that each photographer has an impressive array of "techniques" that separate his or her work from that of lesser photographers. There is more to producing memorable and effective images than simply choosing good subjects.

Ironically, documentary photography's status as an art form was cemented by a movement its practitioners largely rejected: modernism. Much of the early appeal of photography was its modernity. Even as photographers railed against the destructive aspects of industrialization, they—armed with the latest technology—embraced an aesthetic of change that was thoroughly modern. Lewis Hine, for example, was appalled by the squalor he witnessed, but he continued to hold fast to beliefs in the inevitability of progress and the improvement of society. The advance of the documentary impulse ought properly to be linked with shifting artistic sensibilities stimulated by the 1913 International Exhibition of Modern Art held in New York City's 69th Street Armory. Many American artists took it upon themselves to evolve an American aesthetic devoid of European influence, particularly abstraction. The search for "American" subjects and values led to what some have dubbed the "American Scene Movement." Charles Sheeler and Precisionist painters captured on canvas American factories and machines like those Margaret Bourke-White composed in her viewfinder; the anomie of Edward Hopper's paintings are echoed in Walker Evans's photographs.[56]

If documentarians successfully broke free from abstraction, they nonetheless benefited from the redefinition of what constitutes beauty. The "art" of documentary photography is sometimes underestimated because its practitioners were less interested in "pretty" images than in those that were provocative. But the postmodern world no longer defines art as necessarily decorative. Three decades before Susan Sontag made the same point, Walker Evans conceded that most photographs end up as art even if they didn't start out that way.[57] Today, it is difficult to enter a major museum and *not* find galleries graced with many of the photographers mentioned in this essay. Increasingly, Michael Jacobson-Hardy finds his work there as well.

Many of Jacobson-Hardy's photos look as though they are lost images from Lewis Hine's "Men at Work" series involving workers and machines. Like Hine, Jacobson-Hardy works with large format cameras, favors subject frontality, prefers to locate workers in context, and emphasizes strong contrast; he also advocates changes in workplace and society. Jacobson-Hardy admits Hine's influence. He is grateful that artists like Hine have already fought battles over use versus art. But he is perhaps unlucky in that it is harder these days to link photography with social change. As Sontag remarks, "The quality of feeling, including moral outrage, that people can muster . . . depends on the degree of familiarity with these images. . . . Photographs shock insofar as they show something novel. Unfortunately, the ante keeps getting raised. . . ."[58]

William Stott writes that 1930s-style social documentary "is now as dead as the sermons of the Social Gospel. The few exceptions, the works still live and pertinent, are those that transcend the documentary genre."[59] Stott is correct in the sense that photography is no longer a novelty with the power to shock à la Jacob Riis, Lewis Hine, or Dorothea Lange. Jacobson-Hardy states that his intentions are to force people "to take a piece-by-piece look at our system" and to "bring about social change in ways that make life better for workers."[60] Messages must be combined with well-crafted art to achieve authority and impact, but as memorable images from the 1960s to the present show, a powerful image can still evoke strong reactions. Whether they can achieve the lofty goals of their creators is another matter. Photographers like Michael Jacobson-Hardy must actively seek exposure and take their chances with the subjective readings of the audience.

Notes

The author wishes to thank David Glassberg, Daniel Horowitz, and Bruce Laurie for their helpful suggestions for revising the content and style of this article.

1   Francis Bacon, quoted in James Curtis, *Mind's Eye, Mind's Truth: FSA Photography Reconsidered* (Philadelphia: Temple University Press, 1989), 47.

2   Susan Sontag, *On Photography* (New York: Farrar, Straus and Giroux, 1977), 106.

3   The first quote is from Abigail Solomon-Godeau, *Photography At the Dock: Essays on Photographic History, Institutions, and Practices* (Minneapolis: University of Minnesota Press, 1991), 169. Michael-Jacobson Hardy's comment was made in a personal interview with me on July 14, 1993.

4   Although Daguerre gets much of the credit for "inventing" photography, that may not have been the case. William Henry Fox Talbot claimed invention of a nearly identical process and fought bitterly for recognition of his efforts. Talbotypes competed with daguerreotypes in the 1840s and 1850s. For more see Beaumont Newhall, *The History of Photography from 1839 to the Present* (New York: Museum of Modern Art, 1982), chaps. 2–4.

5   Newhall claims that Sir John F. W. Herschel may have first used the word "photography" in correspondence with William Henry Fox Talbot in 1839. Nonetheless, it was not widely used until after 1851 when the collodion process wherein silver salts were used to fix images to glass plates supplanted earlier processes and heralded the end of daguerreotype dominance. See Martha Sandweiss, ed., *Photography in Nineteenth-Century America* (New York: Harry N. Abrams, Inc., 1991), chap. 1.

6   One can trace the shifting meanings of "document" and "documentary" by consulting the *Oxford English Dictionary*. Beaumont Newhall is among those who note earlier uses of the term "documentary" before Grierson, but one must exercise caution in drawing conclusions. Many earlier coinages spoke mostly to the need for historical record keeping, that is, the creation of a repository of images for future study. In 1908 the painter Henri Matisse muddied the waters further by suggesting that aesthetic taste and artistic vision ought to be part of the record-keeping process. Early documentarians often shied away from that notion for fear that art somehow diminished factual content. Grierson applied the term "documentary" in commentary on Robert Flaherty's film *Nanook of the North* as a way of differentiating it from Hollywood movies. Though he too was nervous with the association of "art" and "factual" records, the die was cast; *Nanook of the North* came to be recognized as an "art" film as well as a useful record of Inuit peoples, and photographers of the 1930s began to call their work "documentary." For more see Newhall, *The History of Photography*, 235–38.

7   A fine discussion of Matthew Brady's Civil War photography can be found in Alan Trachtenberg, *Reading American Photographs: Images as History from Matthew Brady to Walker Evans* (New York: Noonday, 1989), 77.

8   For some of the ways in which Northern audiences received Civil War images see Sandweiss, *Photography in Nineteenth-Century America*, chap. 4. "Free labor ideology" was a nexus of ideas promoted by a coalition of abolitionists, Northern politicians, business leaders, and elites in the antebellum North. In essence, it asserted the superiority of Northern economics, society, and culture over that of the South. It argued that Southern society was debased by slavery and thus was mired in a system in which incentive was destroyed, its economy inefficient, its politics controlled by aristocratic elites, and its citizenry impoverished morally and materially. This ideology was used also to promote the "advantages" of wage-earning systems in the North and, not coincidentally, served the interests of Northern entrepreneurs. For more on this see Eric Foner, *Free Soil, Free Labor, Free Men: The Ideology of the Republican Party Before the Civil War* (New York: Oxford University Press, 1970).

9   Although a small number of historians such as Alan Trachtenberg are aware of Brady's antiwar sentiments, very little about this attitude has made its way into the literature dealing with the war. This oversight began early. One of the standard reference works dealing with Civil War photos is the ten-volume *Photographic History of the Civil War* (New York: Review of Reviews, 1912). In it, Brady was praised for capturing images (often at his own peril) but his motives for doing so went unexamined. *Divided We Fight: A Pictorial History of the War, 1861–1865* (New York: Macmillan, 1952) continued this silence, and the Library of Congress's collection spends little time on ideology. Popular works like those of *American Heritage,* Bruce Catton, and Shelby Foote use Brady photos for effect, but spend little time on Brady the man.

10   Vicki Goldberg, *The Power of Photography: How Photographs Changed Our Lives* (New York: Abbeville, 1991), 165–69.

11   Riis's skill as a photographer is discussed by Solomon-Godeau, *Photography at the Dock*, 176. Modern readers are often shocked by the ethnocentrism of Riis's writings. He refers to the "contentious Irish," to Italians

"content to live in a pig-sty," the "pagan idol worship" of the Chinese, and of the "hags," "queer skull caps," and "tramps" who populated what he called "Jewtown." As disturbing as such comments are to the modern ear, they were a staple of middle-class discourse in the late nineteenth and early twentieth century. Riis leaves little doubt as to where his own values lay, even as he lamented conditions and called for reform. For more on Riis see the Dover reprint of his work: Jacob A. Riis, *How the Other Half Lives* (New York: Dover, 1971).

12 William Stott, *Documentary Expression and Thirties America* (Chicago: University of Chicago Press, 1986), 21.

13 Trachtenberg, *Reading American Photographs*, 165.

14 Ibid., 166, 182.

15 For a deeper discussion of criticisms leveled against Hine's work photos see Walter Rosenblum, Alan Trachtenberg, and Naomi Rosenblum, *America and Lewis Hine: Photographs 1904–1940* (Millerton, N.Y.: Aperture, 1977), 133.

16 Hine quoted in ibid., 22–23.

17 Naomi Rosenblum has assembled a useful biographical sketch and chronology of Hine's life and career (ibid).

18 For more on the Photo League see *Documentary Photography* (New York: Time-Life, 1972), 88–102.

19 For Ansel Adams's dismissal of documentary photography and a more thorough discussion of the effects of the genre on others interested in photography as fine art, see David Peeler, *Hope Among Us Yet: Social Criticism and Social Solace in Depression America* (Athens: University of Georgia Press, 1987). The Adams quote is from page 88.

20 For more details on technological changes and the rise of photo magazines, see John Rodgers Puckett, *Five Photo-Textual Documentaries From the Great Depression* (Ann Arbor: UMI, 1984).

21 Goldberg, *The Power of Photography*, 140.

22 Curtis, *Mind's Eye, Mind's Truth*, 10; Stott, *Documentary Expression and Thirties America*, 11.

23 Trachtenberg, *Reading American Photographs*, 190–91.

24 Photography should be placed in a broader context that includes novels like John Steinbeck's *Grapes of Wrath* (1939), films like Pare Lorenz's *The Plow That Broke the Plains* (1936), movie newsreels, the murals of Diego Rivera, and the paintings of Richard Marsh, William Groper, and Ben Shahn. A useful collection of images from the 1930s is included in Philip S. Foner and Reinhard Schultz, *The Other America: Art and the Labour Movement in the United States* (London: Journeyman Press, 1985). Other forms of documentary expression are also discussed in Peeler, *Hope Among Us Yet*, and in Stott, *Documentary Expression and Thirties America*.

25 For more on Bourke-White, her career, and her detractors, see Vicki Goldberg, *Margaret Bourke-White: A Biography* (Reading, Mass.: Addison-Wesley, 1987). Walker Evans's criticisms are recorded in Stott, *Documentary Expression and Thirties America*, while Dorothea Lange's comments are highlighted in Milton Meltzer, *Dorothea Lange: A Photographer's Life* (New York: Farrar, Straus and Giroux, 1978).

26 Solomon-Godeau, *Photography at the Dock*, 179.

27 Curtis, *Mind's Eye, Mind's Truth*, 10.

28   Goldberg, *The Power of Photography*, 196–97.

29   Solomon-Godeau, *Photography at the Dock*, 180.

30   The catalog of this exhibit proved wildly popular and can still be purchased as an inexpensive paperback. See Museum of Modern Art, *The Family of Man* (New York: Museum of Modern Art, 1955). For the record, Steichen and M.O.M.A. curators chose quotes to accompany the photos that had far less to do with the images than those written by Margaret Bourke-White for her work, for which she was so roundly criticized.

31   For images from the 1950s and early 1960s see *Documentary Photography*, a Time-Life book.

32   Many of these images are reproduced in Goldberg, *The Power of Photography*.

33   James L. Baughman, *The Republic of Mass Culture: Journalism, Filmmaking, and Broadcasting in America Since 1941* (Baltimore: Johns Hopkins University Press, 1992), 112–14.

34   Time-Life, *Documentary Photography*, 155.

35   The decline of American newspapers is discussed in detail in Baughman, *The Republic of Mass Culture*.

36   Time-Life, *Documentary Photography*, 212.

37   Sontag, *On Photography*, 4.

38   See Jim Hubbard, *American Refugees* (Minneapolis: University of Minnesota Press, 1991) and *Shooting Back: A Photographic View of Life by Homeless Children* (San Francisco: Chronicle Books, 1991); see also Milton Rogovin and Michael Frisch, *Portraits in Steel* (Ithaca, N.Y.: Cornell University Press, 1993).

39   Puckett, *Five Photo-Textual Documentaries*, 16.

40   Peeler, *Hope Among Us Yet*, 88–107.

41   Rosenblum, Trachtenberg, and Rosenblum, *America and Lewis Hine*, 136.

42   For the record, "opinion" often is accused of being a form of "propaganda," an inherently problematic term given that it was first applied by the Roman Catholic church by cardinals seeking to advance the faith. See *Oxford English Dictionary* (Oxford: Clarendon Press, 1989), 12:632.

43   Peeler, *Hope Among Us Yet*, 78–87.

44   Stott, *Documentary Expression and Thirties America*, 12.

45   Curtis, *Mind's Eye, Mind's Truth*, 23–47.

46   For a defense of Sayles and *Matewan*, see Robert E. Weir, "Matewan Reconsidered," *Labor History* 32, no. 4 (Fall 1990): 629–31.

47   Puckett, *Five Photo-Textual Documentaries*, 40.

48   Rosenblum, Trachtenberg, and Rosenblum, *America and Lewis Hine*, 128.

49   Trachtenberg, *Reading American Photographs*, 200.

50   Ibid., 127, 256.

51   Curtis, *Mind's Eye, Mind's Truth*, ix.

52   *Boston Globe*, December 16, 1992.

53   *Daily Hampshire Gazette*, December 20, 1992.

54   *Boston Globe*, November 29 and December 6, 1992; *USA Weekend*, January 8–10, 1993.

55   Peeler, *Hope Among Us Yet*, 59, 96.

56   Martin Green, *New York 1913: The Armory Show and the Paterson Strike Pageant* (New York: Collier, 1988), chaps. 1–3; Curtis, *Mind's Eye, Mind's Truth*, 23–25.

57   Curtis, *Mind's Eye, Mind's Truth*, 24.

58   Sontag, *On Photography*, 19.

59   Stott, *Documentary Expression and Thirties America*, 25.

60   Michael Jacobson-Hardy interview, July 14, 1993.

PHOTOGRAPHS AND INTERVIEWS WITH INDUSTRIAL WORKERS

MICHAEL JACOBSON-HARDY

46

"I've been working in this factory for forty

years and nobody's ever asked to take my

picture. In the old days all we had were little

fans on the benches for ventilation. . . . The

smell was so bad that it made many of us sick.

Sometimes you go home at night and don't feel

like eating. It'd kind of get to you."

—*Leonard Souccy*

Leonard Souccy (press line operator) melting rubber pellets at Paragon Rubber
Company (closed in 1989), Easthampton, Massachusetts, 1989

48

"So what I tell them, the young ones who come into the mill is 'Don't plan on making a life here.'"—Raymond Beaudry

Lloyd Sullivan molding rubber at Paragon Rubber Company (closed in 1989), Easthampton, Massachusetts, 1989

50

"Everyday, I put the material inside the boiler and wash and bleach it. Then I take it out with a hoe. I came [to the United States] to work. There are no jobs in Puerto Rico. Here there are jobs. If I go back to Puerto Rico, maybe I make $150 [a week]; here I make $254. But in Puerto Rico you don't have a lot of expenses, like heat. Here, I have to pay for my heat. I pay $390 for my apartment. In Puerto Rico I would pay about $130. It's cheaper to live in Puerto Rico, but there's no jobs."

—José Cumba

José Cumba under the boiler where rags are bleached at Parsons Paper Company, Holyoke, Massachusetts, 1990

52

"I've worked in the rag room at Parsons Paper Company for five years. I also work on the boiler and on the chopping machine. Anything they give me, I do."—José Cumba

José Cumba (*far left*) and fellow workers chopping rags (blurred man in photo is known as a working foreman or "straw boss") at Parsons Paper Company, Holyoke, Massachusetts, 1990

54

"It used to be a secure job. Not anymore. The

way things look around here, you never know

what's going to happen to the industry the next

day. . . . It scares me when I think about the

amount of years I've put in here. . . . It's kind

of tough to get a job when you're my age."

—Angel Ramirez

E. Hawkins (fourth hand) and Charles Taft (machine tender), Linweave Paper Company
(closed in 1989), Holyoke, Massachusetts, 1989

56

"I've worked sixty, seventy hours a week at

times. . . . They used to call me three times

in one night to come down to the mill and fix

a machine. . . . I've never been out sick."

—Rudolph "Rudy" Piotrowski

Rudolph "Rudy" Piotrowski (millwright) at Linweave Paper Company
(closed in 1989), Holyoke, Massachusetts, 1989

58

"When I started in the paper industry, it was still . . . a trade. You had to fight to get to be a machine tender. . . . It would take you some= times fifteen or twenty years to get to that position. . . . You had to wait. You had to grow into your job."—Raymond Beaudry

59

Raymond Beaudry, thirty-year president of United Paperworkers International Union (formerly
Eagle Lodge) Local #1, Parsons Paper Company, Holyoke, Massachusetts, 1990

60

"First thing you do is you come in. You check

your whole machine." —Raymond Beaudry

F. B. Wood (machine tender) at Parsons Paper Company, Holyoke, Massachusetts, 1990

62

"It's a dying business now. Pretty soon you

aren't gonna see any of these mills around."

—Eleanor Thayer

Ellery Bunnell standing by the "pulper" at Linweave Paper Company (closed in 1989),
Holyoke, Massachusetts, 1989

64

"They took everything out of the plant and put nothing into it, never reinvesting their money."—Raymond Beaudry

Jordan room where fiber is refined for papermaking, Linweave Paper Company
(closed in 1989), Holyoke, Massachusetts, 1989

66

"There's not going to be that many industry jobs around anymore. We just can't compete. The place that I work, that's privately owned. And someday, when he [the owner] isn't making money anymore, he's not going to run it because he loves us. . . ."

—Raymond Beaudry

Fork truck operator Robert King unloading bales of cotton clippings at Alcon Waste Industries (a supplier of raw materials for the manufacture of U.S. government currency at Crane Paper Company, Dalton, Massachusetts), Holyoke, Massachusetts, 1990

"Millwork has been good to me. It helped me and my husband to raise six children. In the old days, the cloth was so fine I was able to bring home clothing for my babies and fine linen handkerchiefs for my family. At times, I worked ten hours a day, six days a week."

—Eleanor Thayer

Eleanor Thayer inspecting textile clippings in the rag room at Parsons Paper Company,
Holyoke, Massachusetts, 1990

70

"In the old days, we were like a family. People

took an interest in each other. We used to have

a boss who'd come around every morning and

say good morning to us. . . . He'd talk and joke

with us. Now all they want is the work done.

It's cutthroat. Everybody's out for themselves.

The only time the bosses come around anymore

is when you're doing something wrong."

—Eleanor Thayer

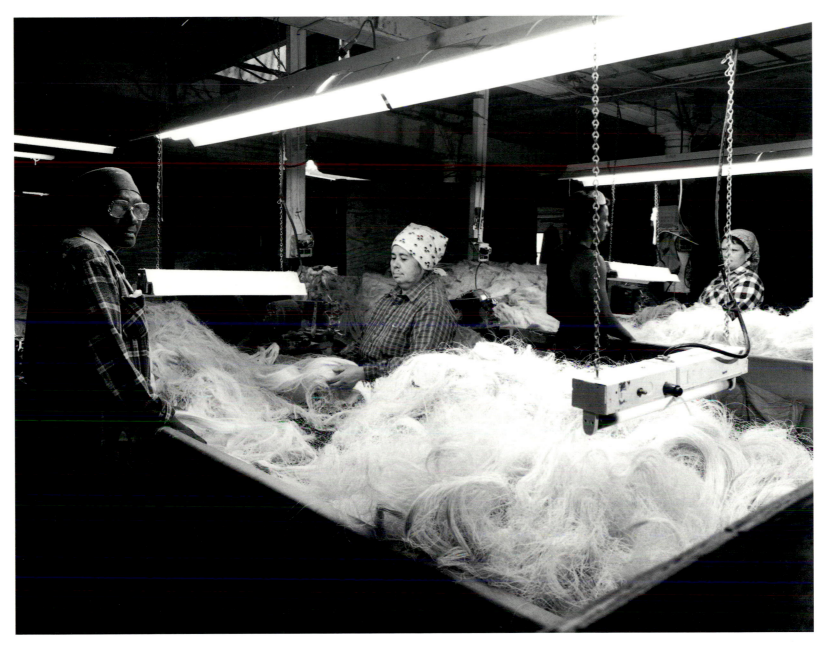

Inez Stevenson, Lucila Morales, B. Santo, Maria E. Rodrigez, Alcon Waste Industries,
Holyoke, Massachusetts, 1990

72

"Working with my dad is an opportunity that I wouldn't have passed up for anything. To be able to work side-by-side with him, you develop a closer bond and relationship. He taught me a lot about the unions. He taught me about all the idiosyncracies of the equipment. He demonstrated fairness to everybody. . . . I later became a union officer myself."

—Edward Beaudry

Edward and Raymond Beaudry, father and son
maintenance workers and union officials at Parsons
Paper Company, Holyoke, Massachusetts, 1990

74

"My father brought me into the factory. He's worked here for twenty-two years. I'm married. I have a fifteen-month-old son and one on the way. I'm only twenty-one. I'd be surprised if the place lasts another year. I may break free and go into the navy. . . . I'm so young."

—Tony Christopher

Tony Christopher (*left*) photographed during negotiations at United Paperworkers
International Local #1 strike settlement meeting, Holyoke, Massachusetts, 1993

76

"Pretty soon unions are going to be unheard of.

Who can afford to strike? Everybody's aching

for a job . . . people are hungry out there."

—*Tony Christopher*

Contract negotiations at United Paperworkers
International Local #1 union headquarters, Holyoke,
Massachusetts, 1993

78

"They don't care about the American people. All they care about is the almighty dollar. You're just a number, a piece of machinery. You've got people here that have given twenty years of service. It's a shame that they don't take care of their people like they used to in the past. Before it was 'we need 'em, we take care of 'em.' Now, they just don't need 'em anymore. Temporaries . . . get somebody else in . . . save the dollar. It's just money. They say the economy's gettin' better, but it's not. How can people buy to build up the economy when there's no work? Factories are moving to Mexico and all over, and the government's just letting them do it. It's just a shame. They should take better care of their people over here."—Cliff Collins

"On strike" at Parsons Paper Company, Holyoke, Massachusetts, 1993

80

"I've worked here twenty-five years and they're going to take a week's vacation back from me. I don't think it's right. They want us to pay more for Blue Cross and Blue Shield, plus take a pay cut, and that amounts to a 25 percent cut in our pay. We're dealing with an outside owner from Delaware and they don't give a damn. If they'd come up and work in this city, they'd see what it's like up here. You've got half of this community on welfare. . . . It looks like they're going to try and put us on welfare too. We can't draw on unemployment, that's for sure."

—Charlie Smith

"On strike" at Parsons Paper Company, Holyoke, Massachusetts, 1993

82

"Ask any old timer what holds a paper mill together and he'll tell you: rags, bailing wire, and rope."—Raymond Beaudry

Back side of No. 3 fourdrinier paper machine, Parsons Paper Company,
Holyoke, Massachusetts, 1991

84

"To run an old factory like this and not keep up on safety is just asking for disaster. Fred Flintstone used to run a lot of the equipment that they're running in here. They're cutting corners where they shouldn't and then they cry about the cost."—Bill Stewart

Metal shafts and waterwheel gears still used to generate electricity and power papermaking
machines at Parsons Paper Company, Holyoke, Massachusetts, 1989

86

"When the mills shut down some workers

never even bothered to return to pick up their

pay. . . . We just lost track of them. . . . What

people got, if they were old enough, wouldn't be

enough money to last for a week. . . . They had

the worst pension plans you ever saw in your

life. It wouldn't amount to a pot of beans."

—Raymond Beaudry

The standing remains of Valley Paper Company on the third canal, Holyoke, Massachusetts, 1990

88

"I like to keep busy."—Janette Keough

Janette Keough oiling textile machines at Harrisville Designs, Harrisville, New Hampshire, 1993

90

"I like the work. It helps the day go by."

—Joyce Davis

Joyce Davis removing the woolen spools from the
textile machine at Harrisville Designs, Harrisville, New
Hampshire, 1993

92

"At one time, in the department I work, they had fifty-four people. . . . They put in a new machine and eliminated about thirty-five jobs. It put a lot of people out of work but I guess it was a good move for the company."

—Angel Ramirez

Loading the warp with thread from spools at Mastex
Industries, Inc., Holyoke, Massachusetts, 1990

94

"During the post–Second World War period, in Puerto Rico you had Operation Bootstrap, which was the industrialization of the island. The result was that people who were living as farmers in the agrarian society were no longer able to make a living. They were lured into the cities for industrial jobs. They were being forced off the land. But soon there was a saturation of jobs in the cities. So they started migrating to the United States. . . . We're talking about unskilled laborers who came to find jobs in U.S. factories."—Carlos Vega

Making American flags at Mastex Industries, Inc., Holyoke, Massachusetts, 1990

96

"Eighty percent of the work force is Hispanic

and they're proud and they're trying to better

themselves. No different than anybody else

in the old days, no different at all."

—Raymond Beaudry

Man repairing loom warp at Mastex Industries, Inc. Holyoke, Massachusetts, 1990

98

"It gets pretty bad here, sometimes. The ventilation system is only temporary."

—Textile worker

Worker dyeing cloth at Mastex Industries, Inc., Holyoke, Massachusetts, 1990

"We use acid to dye the cloth."—Luis Linares

Dye room interior, Mastex Industries, Inc., Holyoke, Massachusetts, 1990

102

"I was sixteen years old when I started

working there. I ran the machinery, made

paper boxes. The boxes would be stacked up

beside me and I would take them down and

put them on the paper; then put them in the

machine that would make the box, and put

them in a machine called a chute. I was paid by

the hour. Then we were on piecework; some-

times, if you were over the daily amount that

they wanted, you would get extra bonuses.

That wasn't too often."—Kay Beaudry

Helen Kennedy has made paper boxes since
1967 at United Paper Box Company, Holyoke,
Massachusetts, 1990

"It's just a job. . . . Somebody's got to do it."

Margarita Sanchez sweeping the floor at United Paper
Box Company, Holyoke, Massachusetts, 1990

106

"It's very fast work. It's a hard job for a woman because you're standing up by those machines all day. . . . There's no union. You mention union in there, and that's it!" —Doris LaValley

Doris LaValley and "Big Mike" Roos making machine fittings at Yankee Hill Machine Company, Northampton, Massachusetts, 1991

108

"It's a very dirty job. When you walk downstairs, it's a . . . big cloudy mist of oil. Sometimes you come home and you're oil from head to toe."—Doris LaValley

Rosemary Szwajkowski extracting oil from metal
shavings at Yankee Hill Machine Company,
Northampton, Massachusetts, 1990

110

"If I ran the factory, I would think about the

people as well as the jobs." —Doris LaValley

"Brucie's Neighborhood" at Yankee Hill Machine
Company, Northampton, Massachusetts, 1990

112

"I've worked as a cable machine operator

for twelve years. It's hard and tiresome work.

There's a lot of walking and lifting and

you have to watch all those wires on the

machines."—Edward Welch

Edward Welch inspecting braided cable at Berkshire Electric Cable Company, Leeds, Massachusetts, 1991

114

"The companies been around forty-five years.

The last five years have been tough. A lot of us

got laid off in 1990."—Edward Welch

Insulation being installed on electric wire (on a converted machine formerly used in a textile mill)
at Berkshire Electric Cable Company, Leeds, Massachusetts, 1990

116

"Where else could I go? I've worked at the

brush factory for eighteen years. I tried to find

other jobs but they said, 'No.' It's hard for a

Polish immigrant to find a job anywhere else.

They would tell me they're not hiring, but I

knew it was because of my language and

nationality—I could tell right away."

—Julia Lecko

Julia Lecko applying labels to brushes at Kellogg
Brush Manufacturing Company, Easthampton,
Massachusetts, 1990

118

"They work the men too hard. . . . They're kind

of rough on them."—Foundry worker

Foundry worker pouring molten steel at H. B. Smith Company boiler foundry
(closed in 1992), Westfield, Massachusetts, 1991

120

"It's hot, hard, dirty work."—Foundry worker

Foundry workers at H. B. Smith Company boiler foundry (closed in 1992),
Westfield, Massachusetts, 1991

122

"I'm tired. I want to quit. . . . I have to work till

I'm sixty-five. Maybe I'll never make it!"

—Foundry worker

Foundry worker by the blast furnace at H. B. Smith Company (closed in 1992), Westfield, Massachusetts, 1991

124

"There are only two shipyards left on the East Coast building destroyers, ours and Ingalls shipyard down in Mississippi. So I don't think they'll put us out of business. I don't really think they will. They could. You never know what a politician will do."—Richard Priebe

125

Bath Iron Works, Bath, Maine, 1993

126

"Employment is very low around here. There's been a terrible number of layoffs. All the work's going overseas. Other governments like Japan and Poland subsidize their shipbuilding. We don't. It's become cheaper to buy commercial ships elsewhere."—Richard Priebe

Shipyard workers tightening the cradle so that it stays with the ship as it goes down
on the ways, Bath Iron Works, Bath, Maine, 1993

128

"They're [the U.S. government] trying very hard to keep yards open but they're getting lean and mean."—Richard Priebe

The ship is held in place by wooden supports. They are all removed before
the launch. Bath Iron Works, Bath, Maine, 1993

130

"I'm a member of Local 6, the International Brotherhood of Shipbuilders. Membership is dwindling because U.S. shipyards are all going bankrupt and out of business. As we lose shipyards, we lose union members."

—Richard Priebe

Richard Priebe, shipyard worker at Bath Iron Works, Bath, Maine, 1993

132

"I build masts and sonar domes. You have to have fabrication skills: You have to know how to drill, how to weld, and how to follow very difficult blueprint directions. We're a group of skilled craftsmen who share a particular knowledge and enjoy it and work it very well. It's a pleasure to be with them."—Richard Priebe

Propeller detail and workers, Bath Iron Works,
Bath, Maine, 1993

134

"I've worked at Sikorsky for thirty-two years. I check out all of the aircraft components: flight controls, final assembly. It's the last step before the aircraft goes out to the hanger. I was an installer for five years, then a lead man, and then a technician. I'm self-taught, I had to learn radio techniques, flight control systems. I learned a lot from books and from schooling the company gave us to upgrade all the technicians and keep us abreast of what's going on. A technician is one step below being an engineer. I'm hourly employed, on the clock."—Henry Phinney

Henry Phinney, check-out technician at United Technologies Sikorsky Aircraft, Stratford, Connecticut, 1993

136

"When I was a child, my father instilled in me

'there isn't a job worth doing that's not worth

doing right or to the best of your ability.'"

—Henry Phinney

Line worker at United Technologies Sikorsky Aircraft, Stratford, Connecticut, 1993

138

"When I first came to Sikorsky thirty-two years ago there were old-time Europeans in there and their nose was right to the grindstone. Some were first generation born in this country. Some were from the old country. A lot of them were Italians, Hungarians. When they had the strike a lot of people came out of the coal mines in Pennsylvania. I had a lead man who worked on the railroad. Now, you've got all new young guys that have taken over management or taken over leadership, and it's tough. It's a whole new breed. They make your life tough."—Henry Phinney

Helicopter assembly at United Technologies Sikorsky
Aircraft, Stratford, Connecticut, 1993

140

"But we all work together and still manage to

get out a fine product."—Henry Phinney

Black Hawk helicopter awaits flight testing at United Technologies
Sikorsky Aircraft, Stratford, Connecticut, 1993

142

"I've been working at M/A-Com for eight years. I'm a technician, one step below an engineer. I work for a wage. An engineer is paid a salary."—Betty Gay

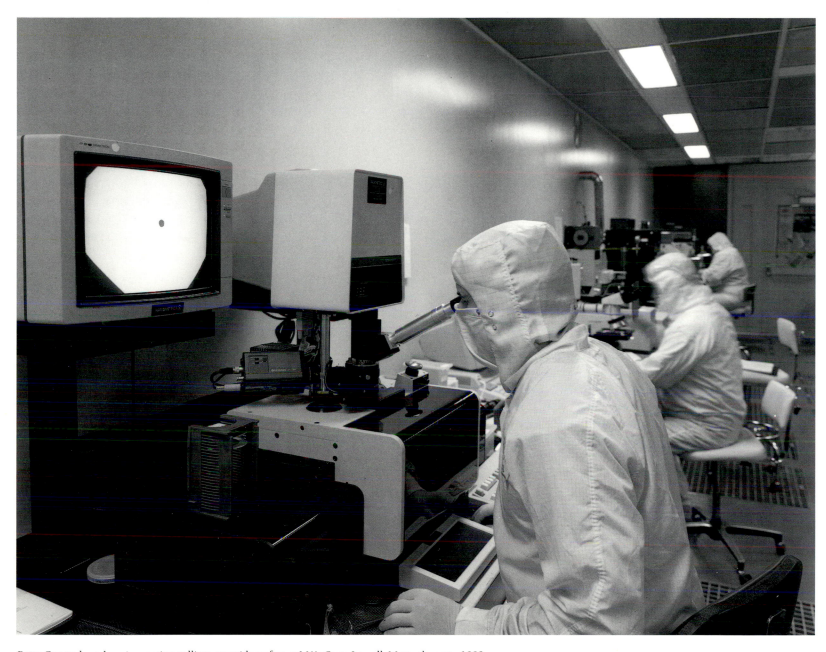

Betty Gay and workers inspecting gallium arsenide wafers at M/A-Com, Lowell, Massachusetts, 1993

144

"The basis of any economy is productivity . . . making things. You take a material and through your labor, you make it much more worthwhile. You can then sell it and get paid for your labor input. We have created an economy in which there are jobs for people that are highly skilled but we've taken away jobs from people who are not highly technical. That means that people who do manual labor are displaced from the work force. You might say that they can do service jobs but somebody has to come up with the money to pay for these services. We used to manufacture but now we import most of what we need. You have to have something at the foundation of your economy. You need a resource that you can sell to the rest of the world. We don't have that resource anymore—We have to make things too!"—Betty Gay

Workers inspecting gallium arsenide wafers at
M/A-Com, Lowell, Massachusetts, 1993

146

"Today they come in and they . . . push this button, that button, that button, and it's going to come out onto the machine. . . . That's all they know. In the old days, you not only had to learn everything upstairs, but then they took you down in the cellar and they explained everything to you."—Raymond Beaudry

Control console at Kanzaki Specialty Papers, Ware, Massachusetts, 1991

148

"When I see too many men on the floor, it

means we're having a bad day."

—Robert Champigny, operations vice presi-

dent at Kanzaki Specialty Papers, Ware,

Massachusetts, 1991

Three-story-high paper converting machine at
Kanzaki Specialty Papers, Ware, Massachusetts, 1991

149

150

"The plan is to do away with manufacturing.

A lot of good people have been laid off. Both of

my parents once worked here and lost their

jobs. We can't compete. I like it here. I like the

people I work with. Three and a half years ago

we had about 32,000 employees—now, there's

about 6,000. Every three or four months, more

people get laid off. It's a slow process."

—Joe DoVale

Joe DoVale moving computer hardware out of Wang Laboratories, Lowell, Massachusetts, 1993

152

"I think a lot of these companies are moving overseas and to Mexico. Cheaper labor. They don't build anything in this country anymore. Something has to happen."—Joe DoVale

Remains of the Sprague Electric Company (closed in 1985). It is the site of the Massachusetts Museum of Contemporary Art,
North Adams, Massachusetts, 1995